UNWINNABLE PEACE

# PRAISE FOR *UNWINNABLE PEACE*

Through candid conversations with individuals breaking their silence for the first time, including key decision-makers and frontline workers, *Unwinnable Peace* masterfully illuminates why Canada's mission in Afghanistan ultimately failed. Tim Martin's groundbreaking work goes beyond the headlines, uncovering the untold stories behind the conflict. With firsthand accounts from diplomats, aid workers, and Afghan interpreters, Martin unravels the intricacies of the mission, offering readers a nuanced understanding of the realities on the ground . . . His storytelling serves as a testament to the enduring dedication of those who pursued a safe and stable Afghanistan, achieving victories in some battles yet ultimately unable to secure a lasting peace.

HANNAH THIBEDEAU, award-winning journalist and Executive Communications Officer with Global Public Affairs

Veteran diplomat Tim Martin weaves a highly readable narrative that combines reflections on his own role as the last senior Canadian representative (RoCK) in Kandahar with those of his colleagues as they pursued governmental objectives set in an inhospitable and dangerous environment. Whether interacting on a daily basis with local Afghan authorities, setting out development projects to build schools and other infrastructure, or ensuring educational and training opportunities for women and girls, Martin and his team forged an incredible blend of professionalism, altruism and humanity in their work . . . It is unvarnished: vulnerabilities, emotions and the cost of personal sacrifice all emerge, including to the present, as the various actors, especially the writer, attempt to reconcile their great effort with a Taliban victory.

THE HONOURABLE PETER M. BOEHM, Senator, Chair of the Senate Standing Committee on Foreign Affairs and International Trade

# UNWINNABLE
# PEACE

Untold Stories of Canada's Mission in Afghanistan

## TIM MARTIN

TIDEWATER
PRESS

Published by Tidewater Press
New Westminster, BC, Canada
tidewaterpress.ca

978-1-990160-34-9 (paperback)
978-1-990160-35-6 (e-book)

LIBRARY AND ARCHIVES CANADA CATALOGUING IN PUBLICATION

Title: Unwinnable peace : untold stories of Canada's mission in Afghanistan / Tim Martin.
Names: Martin, Tim (Diplomat), author.
Description: Includes index.
Identifiers: Canadiana (print) 20240380630 | Canadiana (ebook) 20240380681 | ISBN 9781990160349
(softcover) | ISBN 9781990160356 (EPUB)
Subjects: LCSH: Afghan War, 2001-2021—Personal narratives, Canadian. | LCSH: Interviews—Canada. |
LCSH: Canada—Foreign relations—Afghanistan. | LCSH: Afghanistan—Foreign relations—Canada. |
LCSH: Humanitarian assistance, Canadian—Afghanistan. | LCSH: Judicial assistance—Afghanistan. |
LCGFT: Interviews.
Classification: LCC DS371.413 .M39 2024 | DDC 958.104/7—dc23

Printed in Canada

To the woman who gives me strength when things
are too much. Thank you, Fatima.

When we are no longer able to change a situation,
we are challenged to change ourselves.

VIKTOR E. FRANKL, *Man's Search for Meaning*

# TABLE OF CONTENTS

# List of Acronyms

ACCC – Afghan–Canadian Community Centre

ASIC – All–Source Intelligence Centre

AWK – Ahmed Wali Karzai

BUB – Battle Update Briefing

CIDA – Canadian International Development Agency

CIMIC – Civil Military Cooperation

CSC – Correctional Service Canada

CUB – Command Update Briefing

GRD – Governance, Reconstruction and Development

ICRC – International Committee of the Red Cross

IED – Improvised Explosive Device

ISAF – International Security Assistance Force

KAF – Kandahar Airfield

KPRT – Kandahar Provincial Reconstruction Team

LAV – Light Armoured Vehicle

MPCC – Military Police Complaints Commission of Canada

NATO – North Atlantic Treaty Organization

NDS – National Directorate of Security

NGO – Non–Governmental Organization

PDPA – People's Democratic Party of Afghanistan

PMO – Prime Minister's Office

PolAd – Political Advisor

PPE – Personal Protective Equipment

PCO – Privy Council Office

PRT – Provincial Reconstruction Team

PTSD – Post Traumatic Stress Disorder

RC South – Regional Command South

RoCK – Representative of Canada in Kandahar

ROTO – Roll–Out and Turn–Off

TKF – Task Force Kandahar

UNPROFOR – United Nations Protection Force

# PREFACE

Diplomacy is not supposed to be lethal.

That was my thought as I sat with the leadership of Canada's diplomatic corps at a sombre memorial service for my colleague, Glyn Berry. A friendly, funny and smart man of vast experience, he had volunteered to go from New York, where he was a senior diplomat at the UN, to Afghanistan to lend his diplomatic skill and political analysis to the Canadian forces in Kandahar so they could navigate the treacherous terrain of the Taliban homeland.

An expert on peacekeeping, he was the first Canadian diplomat to work on the front line in that theatre of war. He was killed on Sunday, January 15, 2006, when a Taliban suicide car bomber smashed into his G-Wagon (a lightly armoured Mercedes SUV), killing him and injuring the three soldiers he was riding with. Fifty-nine years old, he left behind a wife and two sons.

I was at home in Chelsea, Quebec, when the news came in on my Blackberry. I was shattered. We needed civilian diplomats and aid workers to go to Afghanistan, to help the Afghans rebuild their country so they would believe in their government and leave the Taliban behind. Canada has the best small army in the world, but counterinsurgency is the hardest kind of war to win—killing the enemy is not enough. If we couldn't help the Afghan people, what were we even doing there?

Sitting in the memorial, I thought long and hard about what we were asking people to do, and what it meant for Canada to enter into hot combat in a distant country. And then the government asked me to go. Four years later, I was to be the last RoCK (Representative of Canada in Kandahar) to lead Canada's civilian mission.

Canada ended its combat mission in Kandahar in 2011, but our military mission to provide training and support in Afghanistan came to an official end on March 15, 2014—Canada's longest war. Most of us in Kandahar left as quickly as possible, anxious to return to our families and get on with new jobs. There was never a chance to process what was the most intense work experience of our lives.

Now, ten years later, the international mission has collapsed in failure and the Taliban are in power. My publisher convinced me it was time for a book that conveyed the human experience of what it was like to be in Kandahar, the difference we made and how it changed us.

*Unwinnable Peace* is based on interviews with twenty-five people with whom I worked: civilians, soldiers and Afghans. Most discussions were conducted online with individuals across Canada and all over the world. I reached out to Global Affairs Canada and they permitted their employees to speak to me on the record. Unless otherwise noted, information provided by these individuals was obtained during those discussions. These interviews were not vetted by anyone at Global Affairs. The views contributors shared with me are their own and do not necessarily reflect those of any government or organization.

Not everyone I contacted agreed to talk to me. The reasons differed but triggering re-traumatization was common. Most wanted to talk. There were a few who believed their careers would suffer if they spoke candidly about their experience, notwithstanding departmental approval. I have used pseudonyms where attribution was a concern.

Of course, everyone who was there has a different story and a different way of looking back. Some of us went out of a sense of duty and to support our troops. Some were curious; others wanted adventure. Everyone remarked on the impossibility of describing the experience to people who did not go through it.

This book has been a personal journey of exploration and

discovery. When I began to write, I didn't know what to think or how to conclude. My experience in Afghanistan left me mentally immobilized by the idea that I might have spent a year of my life on a fool's errand. I've come to realize that there are lessons to be learned and capabilities—like cleaning up prisons and promoting governance in territory dominated by warlords—to be drawn upon the next time young men and women, military and civilian, are asked to risk their lives for our country.

We can't know if and when Canada will have to mount another mission of this size, scope, difficulty and risk. However, the arc of conflict and state failure that threatens global peace and security is plain to see. It runs from Afghanistan through Iraq, Syria, Lebanon, Somalia, Sudan, Libya and, on our doorstep, Haiti. Israel and Palestine are locked in a conflict they can't solve alone.

We could have shirked our international obligations and refused to go to Afghanistan. But we didn't. Being a capable and trustworthy ally is fundamental to Canadian national security and sovereignty. In Kandahar, we paid our dues to the NATO alliance. We also made contributions to the lives and well-being of Afghans, of which some will endure.

I believe examining our role in Kandahar will make readers both proud and sad—angry, too. I am.

# Chapter One

# Tim, We Want You to Go to Kandahar

When you are a diplomat, you never really know where you will end up. There is, of course, a form. The Posting Preference Form has five spaces for postings you would like but, in the final instance, assignments involve positioning, contacts and negotiation.

Ambassador-level positions were official when you got a letter from the Governor General speaking for Her Majesty The Queen. She said to me:

> "Know you that reposing special trust and confidence in your loyalty, integrity and ability, We did on the thirty-first day of July in the year of our Lord two thousand and seven and in the fifty-sixth year of Our Reign constitute and appoint you, Timothy Martin, Ambassador Extraordinary and Plenipotentiary of Canada to the Argentine Republic."

There is a mystique and prestige that goes with the job. The correct form of address is Excellency. For some ambassadors, the occupational hazard is arrogant self-importance. For me, it was imposter syndrome.

Growing up in Winnipeg comes with a dislike of elitism, together with a burning curiosity about the outside world. After a University of Winnipeg geography class one cold February night in 1979, an opportunity to see the world jumped out at me. Simon Fraser University was taking applications for a Guatemala field school that summer. I was accepted and took the bus (many buses) from Winnipeg to Huehuetenango, Guatemala, to learn Spanish.

Fatima Ahmed had travelled from Vancouver for the same reason. I fell in love with her, we went back to Vancouver, got married and started a family. Then I realized something was missing—a job. The Canadian Foreign Service exam was being held just before I graduated, and among thousands of applicants, I was one of the twenty-five lucky young diplomats hired in 1983.

We moved to Hull, Quebec, with our daughter, Natasha. Soon after, our second daughter, Jena, was born. I started out with the Canadian International Development Agency (CIDA) working on the Leeward and Windward Islands program. After a posting in Barbados, I was assigned to aid delivery in Central America at the time of the bloody civil wars there. A reorganization flipped me from aid to the political stream of our diplomatic service. As luck would have it, my next job took me to the catastrophic military intervention in Somalia.

Most of our postings were hard. There was war-torn Ethiopia from 1993 to 1996, after their devastating civil conflict and famine. We were in the Palestinian territories from 1998 to 2000 when the dream of peace between Israel and Palestine was shattered by the Second Intifada and a cycle of violence that continues to this day. We lived in Kenya from 2001 to 2003 where I tracked the fallout of the Rwandan genocide and the pillaging of the Democratic Republic of the Congo for diamonds and rare minerals.

Now we were living and working in a beautiful and culturally sophisticated metropolis, friendly to Canada and Canadians, hosting formal dinners and receptions in an official residence complete with butler, housekeeper, cook, driver and gardener. Being an ambassador is the ultimate ambition of diplomats; I loved Buenos Aires and my job. Fatima did too. Working and living there was a pleasure that we had not experienced before. Our cook was excellent, and after two and a half years, we had each put on a couple of pounds to prove it. Our two daughters were finishing university so it was just the two of us.

My three-year assignment was coming up so I made a telephone appointment with Personnel, hoping to negotiate another year. After my driver dropped me home at the official residence on a warm austral summer evening in January 2010, I took off my tie, sipped a glass of red wine and sat alone in the dark library, rehearsing my pitch.

The phone rang. It was Susan, the head of Personnel. "Hi, Tim. You wanted to talk about your next assignment?"

"Hi, Susan. I think I'm doing a good job here. I like it. Fatima is happy. I want to extend for another year."

"There will be no extensions this year." Then I thought she said, "How would you like Maroc?"

"Morocco?" That was a surprise. Rabat is nice, but my French was rusty and I didn't know the region very well.

"No. Not Morocco. I said, how about RoCK? We want you to go to Kandahar as Director of the KPRT." She was asking me to become the Representative of Canada in Kandahar, leading the Kandahar Provincial Reconstruction Team.

I had no idea that was coming and could think of nothing to say.

When NATO rolled out its stabilization and reconstruction campaign throughout Afghanistan in 2005, Provincial Reconstruction Teams (PRTs) were set up in each of twenty-six provinces as a way to transition from fighting to supporting the shaky new government. Canada was assigned the province of Kandahar, the country's third largest: 54,000 square kilometres of desert and mountains (roughly the size of Nova Scotia), 1.9 million people and homeland of the Taliban. If the Kandahar PRT (KPRT) were a Canadian embassy, it would be one of the largest in the world.

PRTs were supposed to rebuild the economies and social infrastructure as the new Afghan government provided the rudiments of governance to its long-suffering citizens. It hadn't turned out that way. After their initial defeat, the Taliban hit back in 2006; Canada's soldiers were barely able to hold the line.

Canada's commitment to the operations in Kandahar was initially set to expire in 2009. In the preceding months, however, it was obvious to everyone that the job of stabilization and reconstruction was not done, and the mission was faltering. A renewed commitment, more resources and a course correction were urgently needed.

Prime Minister Stephen Harper struck the Independent Panel on Canada's Future Role in Afghanistan, led by former Deputy Prime Minister John Manley, to advise the government on the direction forward. The Manley Report recommended a revamped focus on reconstruction and development.

Harper accepted the recommendations and extended the mission until the summer of 2011. It was not a moment for celebration. "If I can be frank about it, this is an extremely difficult mission. We don't believe it's perfect. We never have," he said. "There has been no issue that has caused me as prime minister more headaches, or more heartache, than this particular mission. I don't think that's going to change in the future."[1]

Implementing the recommendations of the Manley Report necessitated a much bigger team of civilians. Moreover, it meant civilians trained to work with the Canadian forces in a military structure, a counterinsurgency mission and active war zone. Now it looked like that was going to include me.

"We need someone with experience, seniority and gravitas to maintain leadership for Canada's civilian mission when the American surge comes," Susan continued.

Realizing the US had made a mistake diverting troops from Afghanistan to Iraq, and with the NATO military campaign stalling, President Obama had recently approved a surge of over 30,000 American troops, mostly destined for Kandahar, where the main front in the war was located.

---

1. "Harper accepts 'broad' terms of Manley report," CTV News, January 28, 2008. https:// www.ctvnews.ca/harper-accepts-broad-terms-of-manley-report-1.273475?cache=yesclipId-1723871clipId89578%3FcontactForm%3Dtrue. Accessed March 15, 2024

"You have worked in conflict zones. The Americans will respect a seasoned ambassador and we need someone who can get along with the military. You're the right candidate. You'll be leading American civilians as well as the Canadians and you'll hand over to the US in 2011." For the balance of 2010, I would be the Director of the KPRT and the Deputy Director would be an American. Beginning in 2011, our roles would reverse to ensure a smooth transition.

Emotions collided in my head and my heart. "I'm going to talk to Fatima about it. I'll get right back to you," I said.

Fatima was waiting for me at the dinner table. I refilled my wine. "You look sheepish," she said. "What did Susan tell you?"

"They want me to go to Kandahar. They say they need me. It's a big job."

"What about me?" She knew that no spouses or families were allowed in high-risk posts like Kandahar.

I thought fast. "I guess there are three options. You could go back to Canada, you could stay in Buenos Aires or you could go to work at the Embassy in Kabul."

"I'll stay here in Buenos Aires," Fatima said.

Of all my fears, letting my job stick a knife in my marriage was the worst.

"I would like you to go to Kabul," I said. Fatima had worked in embassy administration before and had managed high-level visits. The embassy would need people with her skills. Maybe if we were in Afghanistan together, our marriage would survive the separation. "We should share this experience. I won't go if you don't go."

We sipped our drinks as dinner was served.

"They always say they need you, and you fall for it every time." Under the calm, her voice trembled with resignation and anger. "This is not what I want. But I'll do it."

Again, I was asking her to pay a price for my career. Guilt chafed my conscience. We ate in silence.

A big piece of the Foreign Affairs culture is an aversion to saying "no" upward. Especially when the request is important to your government. This mission was as important as it got.

There was a crying need for civilians to help Afghanistan build a government, a police force and a criminal justice system. Canada also had the commitment and expertise to build schools for girls, bring irrigation to farmers, eradicate polio and promote human rights.

The catch was that reconstruction and development in Kandahar involved enemies who would blow themselves up just for the chance to kill you.

It would be crazy not to be scared. Scared for my own safety and of the awesome responsibility of protecting a combined civilian/military team of over a hundred Canadians, Afghans and Americans. Every decision I made could mean life or death.

Just the month before, in December 2009, a mission to hold conversations with village elders had ended in tragedy. At the second stop, villagers approached and a crowd of kids pushed up against the two light armoured vehicles (LAVs), Alpha and Charlie. The villagers, and any Taliban informants in the area, would have remarked on the two Canadian civilian women, both high-value targets, in the group: diplomat Bushra Saeed and *Calgary Herald* journalist Michelle Lang.

Heading back to Camp Nathan Smith, the LAVs got hung up by a traffic jam on the outskirts of Kandahar city. Reluctant to remain a sitting duck, they turned around. In hindsight, Sergeant Jimmy Collins, section commander of Alpha said, "It was my call to turn around and drive back down that road. I broke one of my major rules: Never take the same way out as in."[2]

The first time the patrol had passed along that stretch of dirt road, a group of children watching them from a distance made odd gestures, covering their ears, but the two women strapped into their seats in Charlie barely noticed. They had much in common and were on the way to becoming close friends. Michelle was telling

2. Colin Perkel, "The Full Story of One of Canada's Deadliest Days," *The Globe and Mail*, December 29, 2010

Bushra about the articles she was planning to write based on what they had seen together that day.

A hundred metres away, a bomber waited at the end of a trigger wire for an improvised explosive device (IED). As the LAV named Charlie rolled over the spot where several hundred pounds of explosives lay buried in the dirt road, he pressed a switch to close the circuit. There was a deafening "CRACK!" and the twenty-ton LAV heaved into the air. Its hatches blew open and its big tires flew off. The gun turret popped off and went spinning away; the vehicle landed upside down.

Five of the ten passengers were killed: Private Garrett Chidley, Sergeant George Miok, Corporal Zachery McCormack, Sergeant Kirk Taylor and Michelle Lang. The survivors were Corporal Brad Quast, Corporal Barrett Fraser, Corporal Fedor Volochtchik, Chief Warrant Officer Troy MacGillivray and Bushra Saeed. After a seemingly interminable wait for rescue, Bushra and the other casualties were evacuated by Black Hawk, first to the military hospital at Kandahar Airfield, then to the US Army medical centre in Landstuhl, Germany.

Bushra's supervisor, KRPT's Political Director Phil Lupul, said, "I can't tell you how devastating it was." His voice was low and sombre as he recalled assigning her to that fateful patrol. "I was the one who asked her to go along with Michelle Lang. And ultimately, the worst happened."

Afghanistan had forced a new kind of diplomacy on us, one that required civilians to run toward the conflict, instead of away from it. It required men and women prepared to work in a conflict zone, live in a military base and operate under military rules, including no drinking or "fraternization."

Physically and mentally, war is a young person's game and I was fifty-four years old. Did I have the physical stamina to work sixteen hours every day?

Besides, I didn't know much about Afghanistan. I had only made one brief visit almost four years earlier as the Senior Director of the START (Stabilization and Reconstruction Task Force), a new program to bring peacebuilding and stabilization to fragile and failed states. Kandahar was a swirl of tribes and clans we had never heard of before, with a culture and language that were impenetrable to us. The fledgling Government of the Islamic Republic of Afghanistan was ephemeral. It could make gestures and assign officials, but it couldn't deliver pay cheques or even show its face in the deep countryside.

Our enemy, the Taliban, were like ghosts. They usually came out at night, driven by a mix of crude Islamic fundamentalism and ultra-conservative cultural chauvinism. Next door, Pakistan provided a cross-border safe haven and colluded with them.

Still, the seductive domain of international relations has a cruel beauty in which ambition plays a leading role. RoCK was a job with a high political and public profile. I could test my leadership ability, diplomatic skill and personal courage in the biggest diplomatic/aid mission Canada had ever mounted. This could be my chance to prove my theory that you could get more peace per dollar with trained civilians than with ever more soldiers.

While running peace and security projects in other war-torn countries, I had encouraged promising young officers to go to Kandahar and support the Canadian mission. Now it was my turn. Saying no would have been cowardly and shifted my burden to somebody else. I didn't think my pride or reputation would recover if I let the government down.

Most importantly, it was a matter of honour that Canada leave Kandahar in a way that was a credit to the billions of dollars spent, the two civilians and 158 soldiers who died (including three by suicide) as well as the countless others whose lives were changed by terrible injuries. The handover of our work to the US had to respect the Canadian sacrifice.

The diplomatic corps in Buenos Aires has a tradition when it comes to departing ambassadors: the longest serving ambassador acts as the dean of the corps and hosts a farewell reception. When I left, the dean was Hisham Hamdan, the kind and skilled Ambassador of Lebanon, who hosted us at his large and elegant Parisian-style apartment in the classiest neighbourhood in the city, and presented me with a beautifully engraved silver plate, another tradition. When I bade our embassy staff goodbye, I said what was in my heart: this had been the best posting of our career.

Packing up our lives entailed preparing a detailed inventory of everything from underwear to personal artwork and family photos. I sold my beloved Suzuki 500 motorcycle. Fatima and I were allowed two boxes of personal effects to go by courier to Afghanistan. The rest went to the port for shipment and storage in Ottawa.

In May 2010, Fatima and I also headed to Ottawa for a compulsory set of "rounds," beginning with the Afghanistan Task Force in the Privy Council Office (PCO), the organization advising the Prime Minister and cabinet. I also met with the Minister of Foreign Affairs, Lawrence Cannon, for a courtesy call. He was very optimistic that we were on the right track and looked forward to building a close commercial relationship with resource-rich Afghanistan as a favoured partner once the war was won.

Within Foreign Affairs, I met the top diplomats and line staff overseeing the diplomatic and reconstruction work I would be leading in Kandahar. Because I would be heading up teams with their people and programs, I also met the leadership in CIDA, the RCMP and Correctional Service Canada (CSC).

As the Canadian PRT would be merging with the Americans, and I would be handing over to the US before leaving Kandahar, I was invited to Washington DC to get to know the US team on Afghanistan. Also, the State Department requested that I complete their management course on how to lead in conflict zones and high-threat situations. The Americans know a lot about this subject—the lobby of the State Department has a memorial with the names of people who died in service of American diplomacy overseas. As of 2021, the number was 323.

During the course, I was most struck by the message that working for a bad supervisor is more stressful than working in a war zone. Working for a bad supervisor in a war zone is the worst of all. I realized that good leadership would have to stay top of mind. I couldn't allow the conflict that had occasionally sprung up between the Canadian forces and previous RoCKs to harm the mission. When leaders don't get along, departments don't get along and policies don't work.

While I did the rounds, Fatima trained for her new job as an administrator in Kabul. She would be responsible for human resources management of the embassy's Afghan staff, for our little embassy airplane that took people back and forth to Kandahar, and for managing the constant visits of high-level officials.

My wife and daughters had paid an emotional and psychological price for other postings I had taken, especially in Palestine. The cost would be even higher in Kandahar so I sought out the Foreign Affairs counsellor for mental health issues. There wasn't much advice she had to give me other than to keep in close touch with Fatima. I promised myself that I would call her every day we were apart, a promise I kept.

I didn't want to talk about the risks with my family and I don't think I was honest with myself either. I was proud of the RoCK job and talking about the feel-good side of the work we were doing was better than acknowledging my fears.

# CHAPTER TWO

# FAKEGHANISTAN

In February of 2010, I arrived at Fort Irwin, outside Las Vegas, for a military exercise called Maple Guardian, a mandatory dress rehearsal to ensure we stepped off the plane in Kandahar ready to do our jobs immediately.

Fort Irwin, the National Training Center regularly used to train US soldiers for the war in Iraq, had been loaned to Canada and repurposed to mimic the Afghan battlespace. Maple Guardian was equipped with the same kinds of vehicles, personal protective equipment (PPE), artillery and communication technology we would find in Kandahar and replicated the austere living conditions we would experience. In previous years, Maple Guardian was held at the Canadian Manoeuvre Training Centre near Wainwright, Alberta. We called it Fakeghanistan.

For thirty-nine days, 3,700 soldiers and civilians would participate in this exercise that tested themselves and their equipment for the jobs they would do in Kandahar. Included in the dress rehearsal were the Canadian Forces Battle Group, the Mentoring and Liaison Teams Group that would focus on training the Afghan National Army and Afghan National Police, and the diplomats, aid workers and other civilians that made up the Kandahar Provincial Reconstruction Team.

To avoid the operational delay, expense and organizational embarrassment that could result from sending people who would fail, candidates for Afghanistan were given an initial behavioural test drive. Bernard Haven, who would go on to work with the

KPRT in Kandahar, described his experience to me. In a freezing cold building on a military base outside Ottawa, candidates for the development team were deprived of sleep and stressed in separate sessions. One involved a hostile on-camera media interview to see if candidates could remain coherent and keep to the government line while journalists used every trick they had to trip them up. Another required solving a very tough problem with somebody who was extremely difficult to work with. "Sure enough, some people went a little nuts. You saw people get very angry about little things," recalled Bernard.

Not everyone made it. Those who did attended Maple Guardian, either at Wainwright or Fort Irwin, where army trainers hired Afghans to be villagers in simulated hamlets and mosques made out of shipping containers and plywood. Helicopters flew overhead. Artillery was set up and there was a red team representing the Taliban that planted pretend IEDs and conducted ambushes.

Bernard was trained in Wainwright in 2009. "We had thousands of Canadians all preparing for different assignments in Afghanistan, all gathering together to learn the wisdom of the last rotation, how things worked, and to give their feedback. This was particularly important to the troops who were going into harm's way." The helmets and flak jackets participants wore were covered in little laser receivers. If you were shot, or the casualty of a simulated mortar, you would be 'dead' and have to take a time-out, feeding into the simulation storyline.

"We lived in tents and we were assigned to a unit. So I was with this little group of soldiers and we would drive around to villages in our LAVs and go talk to the 'Afghans.' I couldn't really figure out what was going on during parts of the exercise. We were stranded there for days. We had to eat rations and sleep in the dirt."

In addition to basic soldier skills, attendees received training in counterinsurgency, counter-IED operations, medical evacuations and first aid. Civilians also learned simple things, including how to get into armoured vehicles without asking how the seatbelts worked.

My training at Fort Irwin was particularly aggressive because the outgoing Canadian rotation had suffered significant casualties. My team and I were chatting while standing in line for dinner in front of the mess tent one evening when BANG!—the laser receivers lit up for half of us. I went to the Chief of Training and told him, "Don't do this to me. My staff won't want to go if you keep killing them."

Many on my team had only been in government service a year or so; some had been hired for a job that they had never done before. Others were from departments such as the prison service or the RCMP that did not usually work abroad in an operational capacity. For them, Maple Guardian was an initiation to work they had never done before. It immersed me in the new and strange world of counterinsurgency operations and how to work with the Canadian forces.

Prior to the creation of the PRTs in Afghanistan, Canadian commanders relied on their political advisor (PolAd) for civilian liaison. A diplomat by training, the PolAd advised the commander about the political implications of military decisions, and vice versa. Canada's first PolAd in Afghanistan was Pam Isfeld.

Pam speaks with a friendly musical voice and her sense of humour is always on. Despite being "kind of round, smiling a lot and not appearing very rough or military," she has had jobs in cold and hot wars, including Bosnia, for most of her career. In 2004, she was appointed as PolAd to General Andrew Leslie when he was deputy commander of the NATO-led International Security Assistance Force (ISAF) mission, was the Foreign Affairs manager for the KPRT in Ottawa and had been to Kandahar in 2005 to cover for Glyn Berry when he went on leave. When the time came to choose a PolAd for the Canadian Commander of RC South, Pam realized that this combat mission needed someone who both knew something about Afghanistan and had experience as a military political advisor. Since that was a population of one within the Canadian government in late 2005, she volunteered.

The Canadians valued her knowledge, Kabul connections and insight into the Ottawa bureaucracy. In her role as political "ear whisperer" to Brigadier General David Fraser, the Canadian commander of the Multi-National Brigade's Regional Command (RC) South, in 2006 she acted as envoy to governors in the southern provinces, pointing out political minefields that could trigger unintended consequences. "In Kandahar, my role was to work operations and find ways to use politics to win the war."

That included figuring out the many hidden and criminal dimensions of the conflict. "It became pretty clear fairly soon after we got to Kandahar that we had taken sides in a drug battle between two opposing Pashtun sub-tribes," she noted by way of example. "That certainly complicated the situation on the ground."

The military's bias toward action gets things done in difficult circumstances. Essential in a war, hasty action can be dangerous when there is not enough information to make informed judgements. Pam cites the example of a 2006 Battle Update Briefing for the American force stationed at Bagram Air Base. The commander was receiving updates on the progress of the fight against the Taliban in an isolated valley that they had not previously reconnoitered. A map was projected on the massive screen in the amphitheatre and on video screens in the other regional commands around the country. Red marks pinpointed where troops were being shot at. A box on the side of the map listed options for categorizing the firefights: insurgency, criminality, inter-tribe conflict, competition over the opium business or unknown.

Initially, four out of five firefights were for unknown reasons— US patrols simply did not have enough information. Watching the briefing with Brigadier General Fraser on the secure virtual system, Pam thought that assessment was reasonable and unsurprising.

The valley was in a little-known area, isolated in every way. "Those Afghans probably hadn't seen a Western face since the Russians."

The uncertainty angered the general in charge. He shouted, "I don't wanna hear fucking unknown! Don't tell me unknown. If it's drugs, tell me drugs. If it's Taliban, tell me Taliban. If it's not Taliban, why are you wasting your time in that damn valley?"

The next day, the map was the same, with some new firefights. But this time, four of the five attacks were not unknown. They were marked insurgency.

"Maybe the Afghans were shooting because they were scared and just wanted to be left alone," said Pam. "But because the blank boxes on the map made the general mad, they changed overnight to insurgent attacks, and this valley got hammered. If it didn't start out as a hotbed of insurgency, it sure as hell became one."

As a civilian with NATO forces in Kabul, Pam had fought to get the call-sign access and radio training she needed when out on patrol, successfully arguing that "need to know" included her. "Will we not all feel like assholes if something happens and I can't call for help because I don't know how to use the radio? Or if I do figure it out, I'm making some major operational security problem?" Unprepared civilians could be a huge liability in the field, so Pam went on to ensure that future civilians were trained in these safety basics when working in an active combat environment.

After I completed Maple Guardian, while we were still in Canada, Fatima and I both completed the training Pam helped to develop. Delivered at the Peace Support Training Centre in Kingston, Hazardous Environment Training is a week-long self-selector that puts you face-to-face with the worst-case scenarios you might find working in conflict zones.

"I'm not sure this is going to be so great for our marriage," Fatima said.

"I think it will be okay," I said hopefully.

Fatima hated it.

Mine Awareness teaches you how to get out of a minefield armed with a pencil. Snaking in the dirt on your belly, you poke diagonally into the ground every few inches. If your pencil hits something hard, it could be a mine so you snake around it. Rocky ground makes it doubly difficult and slow.

If you were to step on a mine and blow off your foot, Combat First Aid teaches you how to apply the military tourniquet you always carry and twist it as hard as you can until the bleeding from your severed leg stops. If there is a big wound in the torso of your buddy, the trainers show you how to stuff it: a large raw pork roast sits on a table squirting blood at you through tubes as you quickly stuff a T-shirt into the wound to staunch the blood and keep your comrade alive for the "golden hour." If a wounded person can make it to the combat hospital within an hour, the chances of survival are pretty good.

Conduct After Capture teaches you how to keep operational secrets like attack plans or base layout if you are captured and interrogated by an enemy eager to know everything about you, your family and your role. Under intense psychological pressure, you must conceal what you know while being sympathetic enough that the enemy sees you as a human being and doesn't torture you. You can give worthless information to seem cooperative, but giving away what the enemy wants is a betrayal of your country and comrades. The specific techniques themselves are secret but I can say this much: the Canadian forces have skilled interrogators.

The last day was as close as most of us would get to a workday in hell. For me and Fatima, it was a mock-up of Bosnia, with specialized actors. The exercise was to find a UN humanitarian worker lost in a conflict zone.

We trainees drove along a winding dirt road through a forest. Along the way, horrific training scenarios jumped out without any warning. First, there was a person stuck in a minefield; we had to decide how and if to help him. Next, the missing person was sighted and fake Bosnian refugees (who didn't speak English) forced their way into the car while the guy we were trying to find ran into the forest. Then came an encounter with irregular forces torturing a villager. Should we intervene? Finally, everybody was kidnapped at gunpoint by an enemy militia and forced to lie face down in a field as the kidnappers barked, "Don't move or we shoot you."

I wish I had had that training twenty years earlier, when I was ambushed myself. It was 1990 in El Salvador when the right-wing government was locked in a cruel and bloody civil war against left-wing guerillas. I was returning from meeting humanitarian and refugee organizations, travelling overland to the Canadian Embassy in Guatemala. As we approached a huge army base named La Conga, we were overtaken by a yellow pick-up truck. Up a hill, we turned a corner and there was that truck, the hard-looking men in the back pointing their pistols straight at us. Our driver had anti-terrorist training and tried an evasive three-point turn so we could hightail it back to the capital but he stalled the car. The bad guys gestured for us to get out.

They marched us off the road, into the bush and said we would be shot. I'll never forget the heightened state of awareness, impotent terror and despair of that moment. I can recall it as if it happened this morning. Then the leader said, "Don't move or we shoot you." That was a big improvement. However, the wait between being told not to move on pain of death and looking around to see if the coast was clear was agonizing.

The trick is to move just a little bit. You wiggle your foot or move your arm slightly. If there is no reaction, maybe your captors have left the scene. Move some more. If it stays quiet, then you very slowly look up. If the coast is clear, you sprint for the closest cover and try to figure out your next steps. Our intelligence later assessed the attack as an intimidation exercise by a government-affiliated death squad.

Fakeghanistan taught us how to work in a high-tempo, high-power military environment. Hazardous Environment Training taught us how to survive in the field. Our departments had been shaped to deliver on our mandate in Kandahar. We were trained and motivated. Next, reality would instruct us. Could we see past the blast-proof walls and steel gates of our base to understand the needs and aspirations of the Kandaharis? Could we reach past the razor wire to build the trust upon which governance and development could be built? Could Afghan voices be heard through the thunder of bombs and gunfire?

# CHAPTER THREE

# THE DANCE OF WAR

Rounds and training completed, Fatima and I took some vacation time to visit family and friends before our departure. Our daughters, Natasha and Jena, came too. When I told my dad I was going to Kandahar, he said, "The British and the Russians couldn't hold Afghanistan. What makes you think you can?"

"This will be different," I said. "It will be about development and helping the Afghans set up a democratic government. That's what Canada is there to do."

The level of ambition was breathtaking. Success required doing three things at the same time: clearing a determined enemy from his homeland, building a new democratic government and reconstructing a devastated economy and society. Yet the aspiration of a peaceful, democratic and developing Afghanistan was shared by many willing Afghan partners, grateful for a friend like Canada to help them take their country to a better place. One of them was Ahmad Habibi, a senior officer with the Afghan National Army who would play a pivotal role in our mission in Kandahar.

Throughout the political tumult of Afghan history, Habibi kept to his vocation as a professional army officer. It is remarkable that professional military values were his compass through the violence and chaos that attended Afghan modern history.

Habibi was born in 1966 during the reign of King Mohammad Zahir Shah (1933–1973), a period that many Afghans think of as the good old days. This era, the longest period of sustained peace in the independent life of the country, ended with a coup orchestrated by army commander, cousin and brother-in-law Lieutenant-General Mohammad Daoud Khan for reasons that remain murky. Daoud Khan established a republic and toward the end of this period, Habibi joined the military high school in Kabul.

After the republic was overthrown in 1978, Habibi attended the army university in Kabul where he specialized in infantry tactics. He graduated in 1983, after the Soviets' invasion, and was commissioned as a second lieutenant.

In response to the Soviet invasion, the CIA spent $2 billion supporting the rebels, known as *mujahideen*, which means jihadist. According to the *Guinness Book of World Records*, the CIA's Operation Cyclone was the biggest covert operation in history. That superpower proxy war killed one million civilians, 90,000 mujahideen, 18,000 Afghan soldiers and 14,500 Soviet troops over nine years. Six million Afghans fled their country to become refugees.

Habibi never fought on behalf of the Russians but a policy conflict between the Minister of Defence, Shah Nawaz Tanai, and President Najibullah, in which he remained loyal to the Minister of Defence, resulted in a period of imprisonment.

After withdrawing the last of its troops in February of 1989, the Soviet Union continued to provide financial support to the PDPA government of President Mohammad Najibullah until its dissolution in 1991. Without outside support, the Najibullah government collapsed, and former mujahideen leaders took new jobs as warlords, the apex predators in failed state ecosystems, able to mobilize militias, control territory and coerce submission by extorting tribute from farmers and merchants on the roads, and sometimes raping their women. Their operations were largely funded by the heroin trade.

Average Afghans were unprotected, abused and ungoverned. In response, a group of religious students in Kandahar organized a political and military movement based on an ultra-conservative interpretation of Islam. They called themselves Taliban, the plural of *talib* (student) and, from their base in Kandahar city, gradually took control of the country. By 1996, they were in control of Kabul; by 1998 they had expanded their emirate to cover most of the country. Ahmad Habibi was jailed again and, after his release, set up a business in Kabul selling boxes and other packaging materials to fruit merchants.

For all its medieval brutality, Taliban rule provided order instead of the anarchy offered by the warlords. They promised to stop the heroin trade and did. That gave them uncontested power to force-march Afghans backwards in time. They took girls out of schools and practised a murderous misogyny. Even so, the international community didn't pay much attention to Afghanistan—until 9/11.

On September 11, 2001, Mohamed Atta piloted the first plane to crash into the World Trade Center. He was filmed making his last will and testament before Osama Bin Laden at Tarnak Farms, an old agricultural research station just outside Kandahar city. His will is a strange document about how to carry out the suicide attack in a pure state of mind and body, with anticipation of the delights in heaven to come. Atta was joined by a dozen other terrorists in a four-plane assault on New York and Washington DC that killed almost three thousand innocent people.

I had just moved from Jerusalem to Kenya as head of the political section of the Canadian High Commission, burnt out and depressed by the collapse of the Middle East peace process and the violence of the Second Intifada. Sitting on the third floor of our dingy, grey old building in downtown Nairobi, we turned on CNN and saw the unbelievable images of passenger airliners smashing into skyscrapers.

The High Commissioner was away from the office that day, visiting community projects on the coast. Those of us in the embassy snapped to high alert and instructed all staff to take precautions because Al Qaeda was present and operational in Kenya. They had bombed the American embassies in Nairobi and Tanzania three years before, killing 224 people and wounding over four thousand. The FBI had used our High Commission as a temporary working space for their massive investigation.

The New York and Washington attacks transfixed the world and tilted the tectonic plates of 21st-century geopolitics toward war. The UN Security Council called on all countries "to bring to justice the perpetrators, organizers and sponsors of these terrorist attacks." This opened door number one: international cooperation to bring the head of Al Qaeda to justice. President Bush demanded that the Taliban hand over Bin Laden and close the terrorist training camps in Afghanistan.

The Taliban viewed Bush's demand through a Pashtun lens. A society known to the ancient Greeks, Pashtuns in Kandahar and neighbouring Pakistan share a language, culture, tribal system and moral code founded on hospitality, asylum and revenge. Bush was not a friend to the Taliban and Bin Laden was a guest, one who had fought with the mujahideen. He had become a troublesome guest, but the duty of a host to grant a guest asylum and protect him like family was sacred.

The Taliban said they were open to negotiations and proposed handing Bin Laden over to a neutral third country. That was not good enough for the Americans and the Taliban became enemy combatants to be hunted down in decisive retribution. The Americans had opened door number two: Operation Enduring Freedom. For its part, NATO, for the first time, invoked Article Five that says an attack against any of the allies in Europe or North America is an attack against them all. Canada now had a treaty requirement for military involvement.

The war began with airstrikes on Taliban targets by the US and the UK. Then elite special forces teams, including Canada's JTF2, hit the ground to help hunt down Al Qaeda and Taliban fighters. While Special Forces and NATO aircraft pounded the Taliban, the US recruited the notorious warlord Abdul Dostum and his

Northern Alliance to come down and take the capital, Kabul. In the south, two Pashtun tribal leaders and their militias took Kandahar: Gul Agha Sherzai brought some of his militia to the fight east of Kandahar and Hamid Karzai came in from the north.

While this fight was happening, the new Afghan government was birthed in Bonn through UN- and US-brokered negotiations. On December 5, 2001, the International Conference on Afghanistan chose Hamid Karzai as interim president. Suave and fluent in English, he became the face of Afghanistan to the rest of the world.

The next day the Taliban told their fighters to hand over their weapons and surrender Kandahar to Karzai. Their spokesman said, "I think we should go home." They had one request: that their hidden and mysterious leader, Mullah Omar, be allowed to live in dignity under custody in Kandahar. For the United States, the Mullah Omar condition was asking too much, so the pursuit of the Taliban continued.

A new Afghan government needed a new army, one restructured from the Soviet style to the volunteer model favoured by NATO. A civilian minister of defence was appointed with a civilian deputy minister and a military chief of defence. Senior officers like Ahmad Habibi received emails calling them back. Habibi was trained by the French army in the NATO approach to leadership and coordination at the battalion and brigade level. The Americans were still leading the fight and planning operations conducted with the Afghan army, but the long-term objective was to transition responsibility for security to the Afghans.

Now a brigadier general, in 2004 Habibi was appointed as chief of staff for the first brigade of 205th Corps, also known as Hero Corps, based in Kandahar city. At that time, the presence of American Special Forces meant that fighting was limited to skirmishes.

As the Canadian forces were standing up their operations in

Kandahar in 2006, however, hundreds of Taliban forces began infiltrating across the Pakistan border toward Zhari and Panjwai, conservative Kandahari districts where the Taliban held the ground and the national government had only the weakest influence. The Taliban were in familiar territory, where they had grown up working in the family fields and fighting against the Soviets. When grapevines leafed out atop elevated rows of soil, their surfaces hardened like terracotta after centuries of irrigation and blazing sun, Taliban fighters crept along irrigation ditches below and civilians left the area, knowing what was to come. The fighting season ended when the dormant brown vines no longer provided any cover.

Brigadier General Ahmad Habibi became our Afghan military partner, commanding one checkpoint in the Panjwai area manned by only fifty to sixty soldiers. There was no fortified base in place for the Afghans or for the arriving Canadians.

In September 2006, Canadian forces moved in on a network of villages from which Taliban attacks on Kandahar city were being launched. They punched a hornet's nest of fighters and were surprised to find themselves in a full-scale military confrontation. Canada fell back before the force of the attack and regrouped in Kandahar with virtually all of its forces, its Afghan army partners and NATO allies before taking the fight back to the insurgents. Operation Medusa was Canada's largest combat operation since the Korean War: 2,200 NATO troops fought a ground and air action over seven days against Taliban fighters dug into the grape and pomegranate fields southwest of Kandahar city. Estimates were that about two hundred Taliban fighters were killed. It was reported that thirty-one Afghan civilians died (although estimates vary), and twelve Canadian soldiers lost their lives.

The Royal Canadian Regiment Battalion Group (ROTO 2 of Task Force Afghanistan) was the first Canadian fighting force on the ground in Afghanistan and carried out Operation Medusa. Their motto was "Who'd a thunk it." Our country was thrust into a surprise war with all the moral and political dilemmas inherent in the business of capturing and killing and dying in a foreign country.

Operation Medusa was a close-run and hard-earned success that cemented relations between Canada and the Afghan National Army. Had it failed, some say the city of Kandahar would have fallen to the Taliban. But Canada held the line and continued to do so for the next five years.

Medusa marked a turning point—it was the last time the Taliban tried to take on a NATO force with conventional tactics. According to Habibi, they took too many casualties. Instead, the insurgents brought some businessmen and tribal leaders into their orbit and became more rooted in communities. They changed their tactics to smaller cells always on the move, using roadside bombs, intimidation of the population, suicide bombers and terror attacks. "After Medusa, the Taliban were harder to fight, and became stronger," Habibi said.

Taliban didn't conduct offensive operations head-on and they didn't carry guns. Instead, they scared the hell out of people with IEDs that could be anywhere and blow up at any time. They also sowed fear through threats and assassination of people seen as cooperating with the Canadians, Americans or the Afghan government.

The Taliban's other asset was money. In the spring, fields would turn pink with opium poppies. At the next year's harvest of the opium collected by the farmers, Taliban taxmen would flood the countryside to take their cut to make payroll for their fighters.

Opium revenue was a reversal of Taliban policy that came with NATO campaign and insurgency. In 2000, Taliban leader Mullah Omar had issued an edict declaring opium to be un-Islamic that effectively suppressed the cultivation of opium poppies and the heroin trade. He had hoped to relieve international sanctions against Afghanistan but wasn't successful. Sanctions were not relieved, and subsequent events were overtaken by the World Trade Center bombing. After the toppling of the Taliban government, the Taliban insurgency embraced opium as a revenue source, alongside extortion and kidnapping.

The Taliban also had a cross-border safe haven. After the summer fighting season each year, the Taliban would sneak back to Pakistan to rest, get medical attention and train. They would bury their weapons or hide them with collaborators and then dig them out when they returned the next spring.

At the time of my arrival in 2010, Task Force Kandahar (TKF) was temporarily under the command of Brigadier General Jonathan Vance, who had reassumed command following the abrupt dismissal of his successor, Brigadier General Daniel Ménard in June.

Ménard had three strikes against him. The Americans blamed him for failing to secure the strategic Tarnak Bridge blown up by the Taliban in March of 2010. Later that month, he accidentally discharged his firearm in a helicopter, an act of negligence that resulted in a court martial and a $3,500 fine. But it was Ménard's affair with a subordinate that got him fired, the first time since the Second World War that a Canadian general had been pulled from the battlefield for disciplinary reasons.

Menard's shortcomings put a dent in the Americans' confidence in Canadian leadership just as their troops were surging in. As a result, they decided not to come under Canadian command, instead shrinking Task Force Kandahar's operations from the whole province to two districts: Dand, which was relatively calm, and Panjwai, on the front line with a deeply rooted Taliban presence. A better general might have preserved Canadian military leadership at that larger strategic level, but it was not to be. The KPRT, however, remained responsible for stabilization and reconstruction efforts for the whole province.

# CHAPTER FOUR

# THE WIRE

It's hard to get from Canada to Afghanistan. After we said good-bye to Fatima's family in Vancouver, we flew to Seoul, then Dubai. After a night in Dubai, we took a commercial flight to Kabul, where Fatima would live and work for the next year.

Dry, dusty and ringed by mountains, Kabul was the power centre of Afghanistan. Like third-world cities everywhere, half-built buildings of red brick and grey concrete sprouted twisted reinforcing rods like cockroach antennae, in case one day there would be enough money to add another level. Embedded in this crazy-quilt urban environment was a huge population of foreigners. NATO countries had sprawling embassies for the armies of diplomats, aid workers, administrators, military attachés, security officers and intelligence liaisons they housed, and the UN, World Bank, and non-governmental organizations had massive offices to spend the billions of aid dollars flowing into the country.

We were met at the terminal by embassy staff and then driven to the diplomatic quarter through busy streets thick with motorized rickshaws. The road to the embassy was lined with blast-proof compound walls and dotted with checkpoints manned by Afghan security forces armed with AK-47s. Entry points to the embassy compound were staffed by Gurkhas, fearsome Nepalese soldiers contracted by multinational companies to provide security around the world. Inside the embassy compound were metal detectors and a Canadian forces detail that also provided close protection for the ambassador, whose residence was attached to the compound for security reasons.

Even in Kabul, the threat level was high. On the NATO base, soldiers carried their weapons with them at all times, a bullet in the chamber, ready to respond to a threat instantly. Pam Isfeld was savvy and seasoned but it still took her by surprise when she was in Kabul in 2003.

When she emerged from a women's washroom to find an abandoned rifle leaning against the wall, she didn't know what to do. She motioned to an Afghan cleaner down the hall to come and deal with it. He met her eyes, then sprinted off in the opposite direction. Pam was unaware of a new standing order that any Afghan seen on base with a weapon, or even touching a weapon, was to be shot on sight. Pam found an American soldier to help her, and the weapon was returned to its rightful owner, who received a mild reprimand.

When an Afghan policeman or soldier targeted a NATO soldier, it was known as "green on blue," something that was occurring with increasing regularity. In 2009, there were five such attacks that killed twelve and injured nine. The following year, five attacks killed fifteen and injured twenty-five. By 2011, the numbers had trebled—fifteen attacks killed forty and injured thirty-one.

The attacks were shocking and confusing to me. Was it Taliban infiltration into the Afghan National Security Forces? Had there been incidents of disrespect or humiliation that required vengeance to restore honour? The threat of green-on-blue attacks added another layer of danger within a psychological climate of ambient violence. The biggest question of all for me was: How much did we really know about the people with whom we were working? Not enough. Maybe nothing. "You can't surge trust," said many an American general.

The diplomatic leadership for Canada's role in Afghanistan was provided by the Canadian embassy led by Ambassador Bill Crosbie, who very kindly invited Fatima and me to stay in his residence.

My predecessor as RoCK, Ben Rowswell, had been the deputy

ambassador in Kabul before going to Kandahar. "I absolutely loved the job in Kabul. I thought the embassy work was meaningful. We were a big player, but we also had real access to the population and it was a very positive time. We were at the height of Canada's involvement and I wanted to stay a second year."

The high-level, high-octane international diplomacy of war, Afghan politics and reconstruction took place at a weekly meeting in Kabul. Ben would accompany his ambassador, Ron Hoffmann, to meet with the US ambassador and deputy, the British ambassador and deputy, the Special Representative of the UN Secretary-General, and the commander of the International Security Assistance Force (ISAF), NATO's organization for Afghanistan.

ISAF was one of the largest coalitions in world history. At its height, the force was more than 130,000 strong, with troops from fifty-one NATO and partner nations. After 2007, ISAF was always led by a US four-star general who directed major generals (two-star), often from other countries, in each of the four regional commands (east, west, north and south). RC South, led during Ben's tenure by UK Major General Nick Carter, included Kandahar, for which Canada had responsibility, Helmand under the UK, Uruzgan under the Dutch and Zabul under the US. "That was an incredibly rewarding experience," Ben said. "Week by week, dealing with whatever the issue was in Afghanistan, coordinating amongst ourselves, sharing whatever intelligence or whatever judgements we had as we prepared for the elections of 2009."

It was thrilling to be at the centre of so much power, to be at the table deciding weighty political issues. Canada was in the game; this was the big leagues of international diplomacy. "We had a chance of succeeding at the Afghan national level. When they asked me to become RoCK, I said no." Foreign Affairs persisted and Ben finally agreed to serve one year in Kandahar in return for a year of paid leave for strategic studies at Stanford University in California. Now it was my turn.

After two days in Kabul, I kissed Fatima goodbye and left her to move into her "pod," one of the blast-proof boxes that were stacked like Legos inside the embassy compound. The size of a shipping container, each pod contained a bathroom with a shower, a counter with a microwave and sink, and a closet, with the bed against the far wall. I worried about her fitting in, but with everybody working in the same place, eating together and hanging out together every day, she was reminded of her boarding school in England. Except her school did not have a bar or permit contact between the sexes.

Riding in a soft-sided vehicle across town to Kabul International Airport, I entered the military gate, where perimeter and internal security was handled by Romanian soldiers, and boarded the embassy's twin-engine prop plane, "the Goose," for the two-hour flight to Kandahar. After pulling up and out of the Kabul River valley, we flew over jagged mountain ranges where snowmelt fed creeks that watered the remote fields and mountain pastures from which Afghan peasants eked hard livings. Moving out of the mountains, we followed the lush, irrigated orchards of the Arghandab valley, then turned south over the beige maze of Kandahar city streets and descended to land in the fortress of Kandahar Airfield (KAF).

KAF blows you away; it could have been a set for *Star Wars*. It is unimaginably big and intimidating, especially if you are not used to strategic military installations. When I was there, it was the busiest single runway in the world with 5,000 flights per week. A labyrinth city of plywood, shipping containers and tents, KAF housed, fed and supported twenty-six thousand military personnel from sixty nations.

KAF was the headquarters of the Canadian forces' Task Force Kandahar (TFK), twenty-eight hundred strong, most of whom were stationed at forward operating bases in Kandahar city and key districts, where combat and stabilization operations were concentrated.

The core of Task Force Kandahar was a battle group made up of a full infantry battalion plus armour (including tanks), artillery and engineers. The engineers constructed defences against IEDs, built bases and designed construction projects and roads. Importantly, they also contracted and supervised Afghan construction companies. The Signals Squadron installed, operated and maintained tactical and strategic level communications equipment and operated special systems to defeat IEDs. The Air Wing flew C-130 Hercules transport aircraft, Chinook and Griffin helicopters, unmanned drones for intelligence gathering and a few Russian Mi-8 helicopters. Special Operations Forces carried out high-risk, targeted operations from nearby Graceland, a base named after the mansion of Elvis Presley. The Civil Military Cooperation unit (CIMIC) liaised with Afghan communities and military police to provide policing and criminal investigation services. Some two hundred medical personnel ran a primary care clinic and a field hospital performed surgery and specialized diagnostic work. All of this was underpinned by a National Support Element that kept operations running. Its work included repairing armoured vehicles, procuring and transporting supplies and equipment, and contract management.

The layout and architecture of KAF combined the brutalism of military function with the improvisation of a hastily built army camp. "I hated the first time I landed in KAF. I saw a sea of plywood everywhere. I thought, 'This is awful. This is just going to be awful,'" said Ben Rowswell. "Once you have a massive military presence like that, cut off from the population, I always had a sense that it was going to be extremely difficult in Kandahar."

With so many mouths to feed, sewage was an issue. On some days, the scent of human excrement wafted over the camp. The enormous "poo pond" in the middle of the base, not far from the US barracks, was the destination for the waste from the kitchens and 1,700 portable toilets.

Whenever I visited KAF I would get lost trying to get from

the sleeping quarters or gym to one of the seven mess buildings: Cambridge Mess was British-style, Far East Mess was Asian-style, Luxemburg Mess was European-style and Niagara Mess was North American-style. Restaurants including Pizza Hut and Kentucky Fried Chicken served up fast food, and Tim Horton's set up a coffee shop as a gesture of support for the Canadian troops—all nationalities enjoyed the iced cappuccino.

KAF boasted a strange little downtown. Surrounding the ball hockey rink was a ring of shops selling souvenirs and gear for soldiers like cigarettes, deodorant and funny T-shirts. There was also a special building for video games to keep young male soldiers busy and happy. Still, it was not surprising that, with thousands of young men living in close quarters, behaviour could get out of hand. We advised our Canadian civilian women not to walk alone in KAF at night.

The biggest security risk inside came from Chinese- and Iranian-made 107mm rockets. The Taliban set them up under cover of night, but they could whistle into the base at any time. When a launch was detected, a siren would go off and everybody would take cover until the all-clear siren sounded. In 2010, a Taliban rocket hit KAF every three days on average.

Workdays were sixteen hours but, if things were slow, staff took breaks in a bomb shelter that had been decorated with a couple of plastic palm trees. That is where our chief of political intelligence, Collin Goodlet, was when he heard the whistling of an incoming rocket overhead. "It was close. And then it hit our camp. I was with a couple of colleagues, just waiting it out in the bomb shelter. And then we heard the sirens and we were quite worried. The rocket hit somebody's room. I didn't know what happened or if there were casualties but it turns out the military member who lived there had just gotten up to go for a pee."

A month later, Phil Lupul had a close call. He was standing outside the Task Force Kandahar headquarters chatting with colleagues when the siren announced an incoming rocket. "The four of us turned to go into the bunker but you don't really get much warning. When that siren goes off, it's already almost too late. The rocket is there.

"I happened to be bringing up the rear and the rocket landed ten feet away from me. As I was going in the doorway, I was hit by this immense blast of rocks and gravel that went right through my jacket and my shirt. For a few days after that, I was pulling gravel out of my back.

"When the Explosive Ordinance Disposal guys came, they said, 'Man, you were absolutely in the kill zone, but it was a dud.' It was completely random, just another example of wrong place, wrong time. I thought of Bushra."

On August 9, when I was still in Kabul, Minister of Foreign Affairs Lawrence Cannon announced my appointment. "Earlier this year, the KPRT transitioned from a military-led to a civilian-led effort, integrating Canadian and US civilians and focusing on the areas of governance, reconstruction and development.

"Mr. Martin takes over this newly restructured KPRT with a view to continuing Canada's whole-of-government civilian engagement. The RoCK's role at the KPRT ensures maximum coordination at the implementation level—combining the expertise of diplomats, corrections experts, development specialists, civilian police and the military—as the United States undertakes a significant influx of US civilians and resources."

The next day, the press was waiting for me at KAF. I told them, "I'm here because I believe we are making a difference and we can continue to make a difference. There's no question that this is one of the most difficult operating environments imaginable."

My first stop in KAF was the Task Force Kandahar memorial for the fallen, a stone wall next to the headquarters building where photo images and names of the dead were etched onto black marble plaques. There were over a hundred of them at that time.

At the stores warehouse, I signed for my personal protective equipment (PPE), the same as the troops wore. Like them, I wore dog-tags with my name and blood type around my neck. With my gear tossed into the back of a LAV, our patrol headed out of the Task Force Kandahar compound, across KAF and then outside "the wire" for the forty-five-minute drive through the bleak desert, past abandoned buildings and then into Kandahar city. Located deep in a residential and commercial zone of the city, the perimeter of Camp Nathan Smith was surrounded by Hesco barriers—wire and fabric containers about eight feet high and four feet thick, filled with sand and gravel. As we approached, steel gates swung open and then shut behind us. I was back inside the wire and on the base that would be my home and office for the next year.

The name of the base honours one of the first four Canadian soldiers to be killed in Afghanistan. In 2002, as Nathan and his detachment were doing live-fire target practice on the fields of Tarnak Farms, formerly the headquarters of Osama Bin Laden, an American F-16 pilot mistook them for enemy fighters and dropped a 500-pound laser-guided bomb from four miles up. The technical term is "friendly fire." Four were killed and eight were wounded. Nathan's photo shows a strong broad face with forthright dark eyes, serene eyebrows curving gently. He was twenty-six years old.

Camp Nathan Smith was nice: tidy, organized and friendly, mostly painted blue. In communist times, it had been a factory for canning apricots. Now the warehouse was portioned into single rooms separated by plywood dividers. I lugged my duffle bag into the room I was assigned, down at the very back of the building. It contained a cupboard, a desk and a single bed. Showers and toilets for me and one hundred other guys were in a building across the grounds.

In August 2010, the Canadian KPRT was at the peak of its capacity with a combined military and civilian contingent of about three hundred and fifty committed to the new whole-of-government approach. Canada had the best PRT in Afghanistan. My American colleague acting as Deputy Director at the time, US diplomat Bill Harris, called our approach "wildly successful."[3]

I was more measured and told the press, "We have developed a remarkable degree of proficiency in how to draw the best skills for this kind of problem from the federal public service and police forces from around the country and have joined (this) up with the military and the coalition. We've discovered practical answers to how to deliver diplomacy, development and humanitarian assistance."

On the civilian side, we had four main initiatives. The Canadian International Development Agency (CIDA) provided development and project management experts in the areas of health and humanitarian affairs, agriculture, education and economic growth. Since the objective was to enable the Afghan government to govern, everything we did kept responsible handover to the Afghan government in mind.

The Royal Canadian Mounted Police led a team of some thirty Canadian policemen and women from police services across Canada tasked with training the Afghan National Police on everything from literacy to investigation techniques. A purpose-built police training centre was established inside the wire of Camp Nathan Smith to protect students and instructors alike. Canada made a concerted and effective effort to include Afghan policewomen in our training programs.

Correctional Service Canada provided five experienced officers to bring the central prison in Kandahar, Sarpoza, up to international standards by improving security, living conditions and vocational training for prisoners. It also meant training prison officials in administration and prisoner handling.

The Department of Foreign Affairs conducted the classic diplomatic work of political analysis and dialogue crucial for

---

3. "Canada's PRT in Afghanistan 'wildly Successful': U.S. Diplomat." Ipolitics, November 1, 2010, https://www.ipolitics.ca/news/canadas-prt-in-afghanistan-wildly-successful-u-s-diplomat. Accessed March 18, 2024,

understanding the political dynamics of Kandahar. Foreign Affairs also funded and implemented infrastructure projects for governance, justice and security. Canadian diplomats were additionally responsible for monitoring the well-being of detainees captured by Canadian forces.

Some responsibilities were shared. Foreign Affairs and CIDA jointly handled strategic communications and media relations, and each deployed civilian stabilization officers to support our efforts in the district centres of Dand and Panjwai.

Whole-of-government would have been a non-starter without the military skills, infrastructure, protection and assets we relied on. A Stabilization Company (Stab A) gave us dedicated transportation in the form of tactical vehicles (LAVs and Cougars) for movement around the province and provided foot patrol and perimeter protection for all our work outside the wire. This was augmented by helicopter transportation from Regional Command South. The Specialist Engineering Team oversaw the design and construction of key projects by Afghan contractors.

The hardest and heaviest responsibility for me and my RoCK predecessors was approving movements outside the wire, balancing the value that a patrol would have for our objectives against the risk of being blown up by an IED buried in the road, hidden in a culvert or concealed in a pile of garbage. This was especially true when almost no one had experience living and working in conflict zones, or even in the job they were there to do. As Adam Sweet, a member of our communications team, observed, "We were the young ones, driven to serve and help where we could, and if I'm being honest, there was an adrenaline rush that came with being there, too."

I wasn't young and I knew better. Having worked to support peace in the war zones of Central America, Somalia, Sudan and Palestine over my twenty-five years as a diplomat, I had seen how those adrenaline thrills often hardened into scars on psyches and family relationships. Despite the best intentions, hard work and smart people working for peace and development, so many of those war zones are still mired in deadly conflict all these decades later.

I hoped that maybe it would work this time. The KPRT was a new kind of organization for a new kind of war. I would work as a peer to the Canadian commander and had the rank equivalency of a one-star general. I would have to shape my relationship with the Canadian forces, take leadership of my bi-national team, forge trust with the governor of Kandahar, work hand-in-glove with the Americans and transfer the KPRT to them, all within a year. All the while, I would try to keep my team safe and get everybody home whole.

I wasn't sure I could do it.

CHAPTER FIVE

# IF YOU WANT TO GET YOURSELF KILLED

It was nighttime and I was standing at the entry gate for Camp Nathan Smith awaiting my guest for the evening, Engineer Abdul Noorzai, head of the Kandahar office of Afghanistan's Independent Human Rights Commission, a constitutionally mandated organization to protect and grow human rights after decades of crushing violations by the Soviets, warlords and the Taliban. I had invited him to dinner. It may seem like a cliché, but extending hospitality and sharing a meal is the best way to build trust, goodwill and get to know someone. It transcends cultural boundaries, even if the food is from the mess on a military base. Without trust and goodwill, how can you expect anyone to tell you what they are really thinking?

I had received military approval for him to enter without a body search. Frisking entrants for guns, bombs and listening devices was standard operating procedure for Afghan visitors, but it was the opposite of a handshake. It signals for all to see, "I don't trust you and I don't respect you."

Entry to the camp for visitors was controlled by a blast-proof steel gate on rollers. In front of that, razor-sharp blades called dragon's teeth were welded onto a steel plate to shred the tires of intruders. The dragon's teeth were sandwiched between two barrier bars, similar to those at railway crossings.

Beyond our walls, abandoned warehouses and industrial buildings loomed in the dark. On the video screen in the guard house, I saw a pair of headlights and then a modest white Japanese sedan emerge out of the night into our perimeter searchlights. It parked outside the gate.

Engineer Noorzai was alone and stepped out of the car. Slender and about sixty, he had a white beard, no turban and informal Western clothes. His face was alert and expectant. If the wrong people saw him enter the camp, he would be an assassination target or his family would be threatened.

"This is my guest. Please let him in," I told the American sentry. The first barrier lifted and the dragon's teeth were pulled aside. The blast-proof gate rumbled open. Engineer Noorzai smiled at me and stepped forward toward the second barrier.

There was an explosion across the street. And then another one. It was an exchange of rocket-propelled grenades. The gates closed immediately. His face fell.

"Let him in!" I shouted.

"We can't do that, sir."

The camp siren wailed and we snapped into stand-to mode, sheltering in place while the soldiers tried to figure out if we were under attack.

"I am so, so sorry, Abdul," I told him on my cell phone.

"It's not your fault," he said. "This is Kandahar."

"Maybe we can try again later this week?" I said in hope.

"Maybe."

I bowed my head into my hands. Engineer Noorzai turned around and walked into the night to get his car and drive home.

There were no more explosions. The disturbance turned out to be a settling of accounts between rival businessmen. But the gates that protected us had closed me off from our primary human rights contact.

As early as 2006, people in Kandahar had started to say, "If you want to get yourself killed, work for the PRT." The Taliban considered anyone cooperating with us to be a traitor. If their identity was revealed, they and their family could become a target for intimidation and reprisal—or worse.

Two weeks before I arrived, the warning proved prophetic. Fida Mohammed had been working at the camp since its canning days. Affectionately known as Popeye, he was the beloved gardener who watered the trees and kept the grounds of the KPRT while his son played video games with Canadian troops. After work, a few steps into the street, a motorcycle raced up to him and two men pushed him against the wall. He was executed with multiple shots to the head, a warning for the other Afghans who worked for us. A bitter chill descended on the camp.

Notwithstanding the constant threat, there continued to be Kandaharis willing to brave the possibility of Taliban retribution to work with us. Before that fateful IED exploded in 2009, Bushra Saeed had such an encounter when an Afghan woman came to see her.

"It was one of my first big meetings and I didn't know what to expect." The woman, a daughter of a high-ranking government official, was dressed in a full burka, her face veiled by a niqab. Bushra stood expectantly as the woman entered the meeting room. "When she arrived, she removed her niqab and had this huge smile on her face. And I was shocked! I shouldn't have been, but I was just shocked."

The woman described the circuitous route she had taken to the KPRT. She had switched cars and "had taken great care to make sure she was not followed. Because she had something to lose. There was a cost." Her smile was infectious and boosted Bushra's innate enthusiasm. "I thought, oh, there's work to be done and the people want to work with us. People really want change, especially the women. This woman really was eager to try to change things and I was grateful that I had the opportunity to try to support her."

To facilitate visits like this, Camp Nathan Smith had to be both accessible to visitors and defensible from attack, a balance that required accommodation from both military and civilian personnel.

During my tenure, one of our Afghan partners came to the KPRT for a meeting on a school project with our Deputy Director for Development, Barbara Hendrick. He was a well-known and trusted partner who had received a threatening letter from the Taliban the night before. Because of the now imminent threat, he had started carrying a gun and asked Barb if it was okay to bring it to the meeting. The military could not allow a gun on the base, but Barb arranged for him to hand his pistol over to the base security team on arrival and pick it up on the way out.

Talking and listening to Afghans about their aspirations, and what help they needed to fulfill them, especially for women, was central to what we were trying to achieve. But waiting for urban Kandaharis to brave the risks and come to us was not good enough. Were the communities captive to warlords? What would it take to extend civilian governance to the districts, each one with a different clan composition? What were their key economic and political interests? This was information that required trust obtained by asking questions and listening carefully to different voices, over and over again.

We made a concerted effort to get outside the wire, to get diplomats skilled in political analysis into the villages in the countryside and hear what they had to tell us under the protection provided by Stab A—their seven armoured vehicles and soldiers were the mobility for me and my team. Barb is unreserved in her admiration for the Canadian military, and the recognition that soldiers put themselves at risk to protect her while she did her job. "Whenever I went outside the wire, I was more concerned about the military than about myself. They risked their lives to make sure that I was safe. I was really worried when they would stop the convoy and send a soldier out to walk the suspicious piece of road and look into culverts and ditches for roadside bombs."

In a land whose culture we didn't understand and with a language that we didn't speak, the success of our mission also depended on the interpreters who were our bridge to Afghans, translating between English and Pashtu and providing invaluable cultural advice. The Taliban called interpreters the eyes and ears of the enemy, targeting them for intimidation and killing. Because of the risks of reprisal, our interpreters each used a nom de guerre. My interpreter was Rambo. His colleagues were Shorty, Johnny, Junior and Elvis. Others were Mojo, Nike, Tyson and Nasr.

Before coming to work at the KPRT, Rambo had been a combat interpreter for the Dutch army in the neighbouring province of Uruzgan. One night their patrol of about one hundred soldiers walked into a Taliban ambush. Fighters came at them from the east, west and north simultaneously. They were hit with grenades and machine gun fire from the mountains above. On their flank, they were fired on from the windows of village houses. In front, more Taliban fighters came at them shooting. There was no way to retreat; they called in air support.

Right before his eyes, three Afghan soldiers Rambo knew were shot and killed. A Dutch soldier beside him was seriously wounded. Wrapping a scarf around his head to keep his long hair out of his eyes, he grabbed an AK-47 from a fallen Afghan soldier, jumped into the trench left in the muddy road by heavy tanks and joined the firefight. When the patrol made it back to the Dutch base, the commander said, "You are Rambo."

Fit and strong, Rambo carried himself like a soldier. His father and grandfather had been in the Afghan military. He spoke excellent English with the formality and attention to honorifics that go with the courteous Afghan manner. His accent was light, his deep voice a little scratchy. When finding exactly the right word for a tricky translation, his eyes narrowed and his face closed, reminding me of a hawk. Working in the field he wore jeans, hiking shoes and button-down shirts, as well as personal protective gear. Off-duty at Camp Nathan Smith, he might be in something more comfortable, like a salwar kameez.

Rambo moved to Kandahar from Kabul in 2008. He had a university degree and had been working in marketing, but the money he could earn as an interpreter with the NATO military was more attractive. He was hired by International Management Services (IMS), a company that contracted out interpreters and cultural advisors.

The year of the ambush, IMS asked him to cover for an absent interpreter and assigned him to Canadian army officer Chris Comeau, who asked him if he would like to work with the Canadian forces. Rambo said sure, but after the Eid al-Adha religious celebration. Chris wished him a happy holiday and told him not to go back to Uruzgan on his return. The Canadians went to the head of IMS and arranged for Rambo to interpret for Chris who was mentoring the Hero Corps of the Afghan National Army.

The work was very operational, and Rambo went all over Kandahar province. When intelligence reports identified Taliban insurgent threats, Rambo would go with Canadian and Afghan troops and police into the field. Patrols moved out at night because that was when the Taliban were most active.

Rambo stayed with the Canadian forces for three rotations or two years. He liked their egalitarian style. Even high-ranking commanders were friendly and polite. He wasn't used to that. "I realized that was their nature. Afghans like that feeling of respect. It is highly motivating."

When an officer put a foot wrong and fell into a deep ditch full of dirty black water while on a night patrol, Rambo jumped to the other side and, holding onto a tree with one hand, extended the other to help him climb out. When the officer returned from leave in Canada, he brought Rambo a thank-you gift—a bottle of maple syrup.

When Rambo asked for a raise, his Canadian boss told him that his salary was up to IMS, the company that held his contract. This was frustrating for Rambo, who was also dissatisfied with the living conditions IMS provided for interpreters: there were no air conditioners in a dormitory where summer temperatures exceeded 40°C and mosquitos were everywhere. Rambo's days were long and started early. "I couldn't get a good night's sleep," he said.

Rambo's motto was, "The harder you work, the luckier you get" so he took the initiative to talk to other Canadian officers, looking for better conditions. He hit it off with the commander of the Quick Reaction Force stationed at the KPRT and was hired to work with him. Canada provided air conditioners in sleeping quarters and paid its direct-hire interpreters $1,500 per month, a significant increase over the $600 per month he was paid by IMS. He sent seventy-five percent of his wages to his family.

Off the battlefield now, Rambo's duties changed. He translated in Sarpoza prison. He went to district centres to work with local governors and accompanied me to high-level meetings with power brokers, chiefs of police, directors of intelligence, City Hall and the governor's palace. He took on more visibility, too. Like our other interpreters, he could wear sunglasses and cover his face with the Afghan scarf that did double duty as a turban if he was translating for me on a visit to a project in the field. But when I was making a speech or attending a high-level meeting, he would be on Afghan TV, just like me.

The interpreters lived on our base, but from time to time they would go into Kandahar city for a change of scene, to do some shopping or go out to eat grilled kabobs. Walking down the street, taking a taxi, or going to the shops, they would all try to speak with a Kandahari accent; the Pashtu language has distinct regional variations "like the difference between Scottish, English and Canadian accents." Whenever he was talking to Kandaharis, he was friendly and funny to allay suspicion.

The Taliban were everywhere and could strike at any time, just as the mujahideen had done in their fight against the Soviets, who had called them "ghosts." Invisible to us, they could be in any district, any village and any house. As Rambo explained, "You didn't know who was Talib because you talked with fifty people from one village where last week you got ambushed. So you didn't know how many Talibs you were speaking with. They all had the same turbans." With jobs like interpreting in the prison, he was face-to-face with Taliban fighters and it could be scary. "You never knew when that detainee was coming out of the jail. And if they found out who you were, there was no going back."

# CHAPTER SIX

# BATTLE RHYTHM

When I arrived at Camp Nathan Smith, my top priority was to establish a strong working relationship with the Canadian forces. Had Stab A been reassigned to support the main effort in Panjwai, we would have been unable to do our job, our relevance leaking away while we waited to close the mission and the Americans ramped up to take over.

Ben Rowswell had had a difficult time working with Ménard. Ménard did not demonstrate cooperation or respect for the civilian team and his commanders picked up that attitude. Ben recalls a briefing of the Minister of Defence by the major of a forward operating base who said, "Afghans are so primitive, they don't understand human rights, they don't understand democracy. All they understand is power and stability. And they want someone strong to assure them that they're going to be safe and to make sure that there are jobs. They don't want any of this other stuff." After the deadly attack of December 30, 2009, relations became even more strained and projects lost momentum.

I didn't know things had been so bad before my arrival. But I did know that my relationship with Brigadier General Dean Milner, appointed commander the month after I took up my post, would be absolutely critical to my success.

In Canada, a couple of beers would have been the default way for Dean and me to get to know each other. That was not an option in Kandahar, where beer and wine were restricted to a monthly event at which each soldier or civilian was allowed two beers or a bottle of wine to share with another person. In the absence of alcohol to lighten inhibitions and smooth social relations, military officers smoke cigars. Dean invited me for a cigar behind our sleeping quarters after work one evening when I was spending the night at KAF. There were a couple of beach chairs in the yard to take in the night air and, for a change, we had the evening to ourselves. Dean had good cigars.

Dean had been eager to go to Afghanistan. The final tour of Task Force Kandahar was the last foreseeable chance to command troops in battle and, as such, would be the worthy culmination of a remarkable career. In 1994, then-Major Milner commanded men as part of UNPROFOR (United Nations Protection Force), a peacekeeping mission to stabilize the multiple crises and violence stemming from the collapse of Yugoslavia. In November of that year, a bunch of mercenaries fighting for the Serbs known as the Iljisa Brigade captured Dean and fifty-five of his soldiers from the Royal Canadian Dragoons A squadron. They were held incommunicado for fifteen days.

Strength and size matter in peacekeeping and Dean had neither in Bosnia. In a notorious incident the next year, a lightly armed Dutch army formation of 370 soldiers was initially deployed to enforce a safe zone for the community of Srebrenica but failed to deter the Scorpions, a paramilitary force loyal to the government of Serbia that killed some eight thousand Bosnian Muslim men and boys. It was an act of genocide that a weak peacekeeping force was unable to prevent. Dean told me, "When I was first on the ground, UNPROFOR had a very weak mandate. We were essentially along the line of confrontation and we were observing, but we didn't have robust enough Rules of Engagement to be able to do much. We did get in the way, but there was an understanding that with the atrocities and the ethnic cleansing that was happening, the mission needed to evolve."

In 2000, Dean was a senior officer in the UN peacekeeping

operation maintaining the ceasefire between Eritrea and Ethiopia. It was one of the last classic types of peacekeeping operations, separating two United Nations member states who could not stop themselves from falling into a stupid, costly and deadly conflict. That mission lasted from 2000 to 2008 and was successful in creating conditions for the two countries to disengage and stop fighting.

From 2005 to 2007, Colonel Milner was the Director of Army Training responsible for collective training that included preparing Battle Groups for Afghanistan. From 2007 to 2009, he commanded 2 Canadian Mechanized Brigade Group in Petawawa, Ontario, and was responsible for training and preparing the 3rd Battalion of the Royal Canadian Regiment for their deployment to Afghanistan as Task Force ROTO 6. By 2009, he was preparing the 1st Battalion of the Royal Canadian Regiment Battle Group for the ninth rotation of Task Force Kandahar (ROTO 9), a role that left him frustrated. "You do all that training and then you don't deploy. We had a system where we wanted the brigade commander to focus on the training, and then he would go over with another headquarters. I felt it was difficult to send the troops off and not be going myself because I like operations." By operations, he meant expeditionary missions leading combat-capable troops in geostrategically critical conflicts.

His frustration didn't last long. About six months after sending ROTO 9 to Kandahar, the Commander of Land Forces, Lieutenant General Andrew Leslie, drove 163 kilometres north from Ottawa to Petawawa to say, "You're the leader we want to go."

Dean felt ready. He was professionally prepared and personally excited. He liked the mission and he liked that Canada had a big tough piece of the fight. "I was prepared in all facets, whole-of-government, counterinsurgency, warfighting," he said. At the same time, it made for a tough conversation with his wife Katrin and teenage son and daughter, especially after what he and they had gone through in Bosnia. They knew it would be dangerous because his operational style was to be on the ground constantly, close to the fight. He understood the unconditional source of strength families provide to soldiers in a theatre of war. "All that to say, my family was very supportive and very worried."

It was good to talk about our families and share the concerns that come from being far away in a war zone. That cigar was a gesture of friendship, and getting to know Dean as a person opened a path to the trust we would need to work together. He gave me my first nickname: Timmer.

It takes a lot of soldiers spread out among villages and living with the population to separate insurgents from their communities. The Taliban were rooted in rural Pashtu culture in complex ways, from religion to justice to tribal affiliations.

To fight an invisible enemy, Dean would need someone with both academic qualifications and street cred to advise on counter-insurgency, someone to help him navigate the murky human terrain that was the Kandahar battlefield. What were the implications of moving into this village or that one? Which tribal leader could be trusted? Which one had ties to the enemy?

A civilian professor had been selected for the role of counter-insurgency advisor but, a young father with a new family, had pulled out for safety reasons. Dean's choice for a replacement was Howard Coombs. Coombs had been in Kabul at the beginning, a major serving on the NATO Strategic Advisory Team deployed to stabilize the nation after the Taliban were toppled in 2004. He knew Afghanistan well. Now a civilian, he and Dean had been captains together. Dean trusted him.

The two men, accompanied by their wives, met again at a formal dinner before Dean shipped out. Dean was about to be promoted from Colonel to Brigadier General and was putting together his leadership team. As the two couples chatted in their formal wear, Dean suggested that Howard fill the vacant advisor position.

Howard's wife, Donna, looked at him and, in a deadly serious voice, told Dean, "He's not going anywhere."

Dean requested Howard anyway and Howard received a letter telling him that he was going to Kandahar. He accepted the job even though "there was some friction at the house for a couple of days. Then Donna said 'Okay, if you really want to do this thing, I'll be behind you.'"

Her fears, like those of Dean's family, were well-founded. As Dean and Howard accompanied an early foot patrol in the forward part of a single-file formation going through the countryside, a hidden fighter detonated an IED fifteen feet in front of them. The IED was designed and planted with directions in mind—two shotgun shells the size of scuba tanks pointing up and down the road and could have wiped out the whole patrol. Amazingly, there were no casualties—the detonator went off but did not trigger the main explosives because of moisture in the blast cap.

It was a seminal moment for Howard. "I realized at that moment the nature of the leadership that Dean was going to have to exert. The whole operation demanded his presence."

A couple of days later they patrolled again and found another IED, this time before it detonated. The Taliban were trying to get Dean, the new Canadian general.

On other occasions, Dean took calculated risks to get close to the Kandahari people. As he was doing foot patrols, getting to know the place, he said, "I went right into Panjwai town, right into the district centre. And I spoke to a whole bunch of people. And I'm looking in the crowd—I mean, I've got some tough-looking buggers—I just did not know if I could walk anywhere. You could never tell who the enemy was." In all, Dean clocked 14,000 kilometres on his LAV moving across the theatre of operations, maintaining a detailed situational awareness and keeping in touch with the Afghan leaders in his area.

Like Dean, I enjoyed going outside the wire. We had projects all over Kandahar city and the province, and there was no substitute for first-hand visits to get a handle on what we were doing and how it was going. Every week, I would have meetings in the districts up and down the valley. If it was in Dean's districts (Dand and Panjwai) we would usually be together. Dand was close enough to travel by road. If it was Panjwai, farther away and on the front line, my KPRT colleagues and I would go by helicopter, either an American Black Hawk or a Canadian Chinook.

Howard believes the forward presence of both civilian and military leaders was critical. "The presence you and Dean provided by going out all the time, particularly in district centres, made a significant impact on operations in Kandahar." It showed support for the Afghans and modelled the close relationship we needed to have across our organizations, especially as military and civilian time scales don't naturally mesh.

The military was looking for quick impact benefits—they thought if the aid came quickly, soon after a community was cleared of the Taliban by military operations, then people would associate the aid with the military and shift loyalty away from the Taliban. Our aid programs didn't work that way. They were slow and required planning and community consultation, which led to military frustration. They thought the civilian side was not helping the counterinsurgency effort.

Battle rhythm is the pulse of military operations. It is intensive, demanding and repeats at exactly the same time each day, anchored by the morning Commander Update Briefing (CUB) and the evening Battle Update Briefing (BUB). Held at Task Force Kandahar headquarters at KAF with video links to forward operating bases like Camp Nathan Smith, the CUB and the BUB occurred at a big U-shaped table with the commander in the centre. The chairs on either side were arrayed according to the Napoleonic staffing system that is still utilized by NATO. Around the table would be the commander of J1 (personnel), J2 (intelligence), J3 (operations) and so forth. Bernard Haven, our Senior Development Officer, was initially posted to KAF as a civilian advisor to RC South. He recalls that, "Everybody had a place and knew what to do, except the civilians, who had to figure out where to sit."

All aspects of operations were covered, everything from troops in contact, casualties and the health of the troops to logistics like delivery of food and water. Sometimes the chaplain provided a briefing on the morale of the soldiers. The amount of information was vast and the acronyms were confusing. To stay connected, Dean assigned Colonel Louis Cyr as my liaison. Through Louis I could get messages to Dean; he could put them in the language that meshed with Task Force Kandahar operations and vice versa.

I would go to KAF every couple of weeks where the Commander of RC South regularly convened the commanders in Southern Afghanistan for the rollout of strategic plans or updates on how the war was going. I would be speaking for the KPRT, providing updates on the progress and problems of governance and development. KAF was also the address for high-level meetings with American representatives and Task Force Kandahar, especially Dean and Howard.

Life at the KPRT was also regimented. Up at six, I would drag on my gym shorts and shirt, slide into a pair of flip flops, grab my sponge bag and towel then, bleary-eyed, pad down the long dark hall of our warehouse/dormitory as the other occupants, mostly military personnel from Canadian and American units, did the same. Walking into the sunlight and down a cement ramp that opened into the yard, I would shuffle through the chilly dawn across the dusty gravel to the toilet and shower facilities: a long row of sinks against the blue wall on one side, behind that a long row of toilets and beyond that shower stalls with benches to change. It was steamy and crowded.

Back in my room, I would hang up my towel and pull on my work clothes. Passing by the mess to fill my steel mug with coffee,

I would switch on the first of my three communications systems: my Foreign Affairs MS Outlook system gave me unclassified and personal coms. Locked up in the filing cabinet was the hard drive for the classified system we used for sensitive subjects like detainee reports. Then there was a hardened Toshiba laptop connected to the Canadian forces' system, cased in steel to survive the hard knocks of battlefield use. It was used for anything that involved operational security, such as patrol routes and timing.

The day started with our Operations meeting. I would sit next to my US colleague, Bill Harris, a veteran American diplomat widely respected for his knowledge and skill in operating in the counterinsurgency environment of Kandahar. We were flanked by Bill's Chief of Staff, Jason, and my Chief of Staff, Doug. Phil Lupul and Greg Galligan, both from the political section, operated as a Canadian unit. So did the civilian police and corrections team. The development professionals were functionally integrated, with a dozen Canadian and American colleagues interspersed around the table, clustered in sectors like education, economic growth, health, water and agriculture. Colonel Louis Cyr joined us to make sure our work was connected and coordinated with Task Force Kandahar. Rapid fire briefings and feedback gave me and everyone else the information we needed on what was happening that day.

In total, there were seventy-five civilians stationed at Camp Nathan Smith, along with almost three hundred troops, both Canadian and American. Not surprisingly, it was an overwhelmingly male environment. But that didn't make it threatening for women. Katherine Heath-Eves, one of our communications professionals, said, "In some respects, it was kind of like being the head cheerleader. When you walked through the cafeteria or around the base, you did feel that all the eyes were on you. There's a vulnerability to that, but there's also kind of a flattery that I hadn't experienced working in Canada."

A classic beauty with blond hair and blue eyes, Katherine was careful about her appearance. "The clothes we wear communicate something about us. As a young woman living in a military base in a war zone, I would never wear anything revealing. I tried to dress on-point with how the military dressed, but a civilian version of that. Khakis and button-up shirts. Outside the wire, I wore a scarf. No jewellery."

The women on our team found a look that was professional and appropriate for throwing on a flak jacket and helmet. Seeing women on temporary duty who dressed inappropriately made them angry. "As civilians," Katherine said, "we wanted to show respect for the military environment in which we were working."

In general, the women were also respected by Afghan men. "They just didn't know what to do with the woman in the mix," Katherine explained. "I guess they saw me as an alien. I felt like I was gender-less with most of them." Unfortunately, one of the interpreters developed a crush and gave Katherine a necklace with a message of love written on it. "I think he had built up a whole world in his head about what would happen in that moment." After she told him, "Sorry, but this relationship is not going to happen," the awkwardness lingered throughout her posting.

Most days I had ground movements, usually with other members of the team and Rambo. Ground movements started with Orders, a briefing on logistics. Ty, the Canadian soldier assigned as my bodyguard, and I would walk to the assembly point where the vehicles idled patiently and the others on the patrol stood waiting. Wiry, alert and quiet, Ty and his SIG Sauer automatic pistol were by my side whenever I went outside the wire. I never doubted for a second that he would risk his life to save mine. The patrol leader would explain the route we would be taking and the order of march that established which vehicles were in the front, middle and rear. The arrival procedure and security at the destination would be explained, too.

Frequent destinations in Kandahar city were the governor's palace, city hall, Sarpoza prison, the National Directorate of Security, Kandahar Police Headquarters, the Provincial Council and Kandahar University.

When I returned to the KPRT, it would be time to feed the beast—the government policymaking and communications machine that lived on the mass of reports we constantly submitted through military and civilian channels. There were political reports, input on intelligence analyses, progress indicators for NATO, weekly situation reports bringing together the work of all lines of business that went out every Friday. High-level visits required reports to Ottawa. The Governor General, Prime Minister, Minister of Defence (multiple times) and the Minister of International Development all came. American national security advisors, senators and congressmen plus NATO commanders came through, all requiring high-level briefings and follow-up reporting.

After a break for dinner, it was time for my intelligence briefing. Often at 8:00 p.m. my Secure Telephone Unit rang. The STUIII provides phone-to-phone encryption of voice, permitting discussions at the level of top secret. That was how I kept in sync with decision-makers in Privy Council Office, Foreign Affairs and the CIDA. Before bed, I would go to a quiet corner of the base behind the mechanics shop to call Fatima. I told her what I could, knowing that whatever we said on our unsecured line would be captured by one intelligence agency or another.

The Americans started taking over the management of the base just as I arrived. While I was Director of the KPRT and responsible for our Canadian civilian work, Camp Nathan Smith became the base for the US combat effort in Kandahar city. The character of the base changed. At least a thousand troops flooded into an area the size of a few city blocks. Buildings and tents sprouted up in vacant spaces. Food became more American. Coffee got worse and the bathroom got very crowded.

A plywood amphitheatre was constructed with video consoles used for CUBs and BUBs. I skipped the morning CUBs—they weren't necessary for me—but I attended the BUBs, led by General Terry, the new commander of RC South, who was dialled in from his KAF headquarters. All the district commanders of the south— Kandahar, Helmand, Uruzgan and Zabul—reported in on a daily basis. The room was full of dozens of military staff. It was like drinking from a firehose but was good for my situational awareness of what was happening with the military campaign across Kandahar province. It helped me find a way to shoehorn our civilian work into the prosecution of the biggest NATO operation ever.

# CHAPTER SEVEN

# HAMKARI

It was a bit of a struggle to get my flak jacket over my navy blue suit and tie. The coat got wrinkled and the hiking boots looked out of place. Never mind, I told myself, the black loafers would have become covered in dust walking across the base, anyway. Formality is a sign of respect in diplomacy, so I wanted to dress the part for my first meeting outside the wire, with Governor Tooryalai (Toor) Wesa.

Toor lived in a large, low palace in the centre of town, its perimeter tightly secured by US and Afghan soldiers and police. We entered the main gates into a green courtyard surrounded by palm trees and enlivened by a burbling fountain. The imposing veranda was some forty metres wide. Escorted by Ty, I climbed low stairs and passed under the pointed crowns of fortress-thick ogival arches into the welcome shade of a receiving porch, then through reinforced doors into the waiting rooms, meeting rooms and finally into Toor's office. The private residence he shared with his wife, Rangina, was in the back.

I stepped into his large office as Ty stood watchfully in a corner. Toor stood up to shake my hand. He wore a beige salwar kameez with a dark vest and leather sandals. He did not have a beard or an elder's turban. His bearing was measured and dignified.

First courtesy calls only happen once. It was a time for me to listen, give the governor a chance to know me and tell me what I needed to know. My only objective was building trust. Toor had a reputation for being tough and critical of Canada. Hearing about

61

his meetings with Ben, Toor often complained about Canada. "You make promises and you do nothing," he would say. The criticism was unrelenting, and sometimes he was right. He worried that the big Dahla Dam project needed trained experts to run it and successfully insisted that a high-level training program be added.

I told Toor about my ambassadorial experience and familiarity with conflict zones. I told him about Fatima and my daughters so he could get a sense of my life outside work. "Your success is my objective," I said. "Let's keep a direct line of communication open."

Toor got down to business. "People need to see benefits from Canadian projects. Use local Kandahari contractors, I can help you with that." With all the aid coming into Kandahar from Canada and the US, who got contracting money made a big difference. Allocation of contracts could buy political support and reinforce security, or it could create grievances and conflict. Toor needed to manage this, but with so much corruption around, I had to assign contracts by the book, and I told him that.

NATO had just initiated a new strategic operation for Kandahar called Operation Hamkari. Hamkari means "cooperation" and the idea was that everything we did was to be done through the provincial government, as opposed to foreigners. Having made the strategic commitment to give Toor this influence, we also gave him power and control, which invited a challenge for us. Hamkari added a new accountability for the performance of the KPRT to Toor and, through him, to the people of Kandahar.

Toor's predecessor, Assadullah Khalid, was a dashing young figure given to wearing designer jeans and a sidearm who clung to bitterly contested reins of power by relying on improvised alliances fuelled by money. With no functioning police force or justice system, expediency was the only option available. Corruption and incompetence, enabled by widespread illiteracy, were the norm. Hands got very dirty and getting it wrong got leaders killed.

It wasn't Canada's job to choose the Afghan leaders we worked with, and Assadullah was a good military partner who leaned into the fight against the Taliban. Prior to Operation Medusa, Assadullah told the Canadian commander which local leaders were in cahoots with the Taliban. When Pam Isfeld was in Kandahar in 2006, Assadullah showed up at the Canadian headquarters on a horse and said he was going to chase a pack of Taliban fighters hiding in the nearby mountains. A detachment of Canadian soldiers joined the posse.

Assadullah seemed a good enough governor until his disregard for human rights fuelled a political firestorm. In April 2007, *The Globe and Mail* reported that Afghan officials tortured their captives.[4] Canadian documents referred to Assadullah's reputation as that of a "sexual predator and drug user"[5] and a Canadian corrections official interviewed a prisoner who claimed that Assadullah had personally beaten him and administered electric shocks during an interrogation.[6]

In an interview, a source who served on Canada's headquarters staff said he heard a story of torture from Assadullah's own mouth. Afghan authorities were trying to decide whether to pay compensation to a man from an outlying district who claimed his brother was killed during interrogation. The governor acknowledged causing the man's death, the source said. The matter was solved in the traditional way and the victim's brother received a sum equivalent to roughly US$2,000.

Rick Hillier, Canada's Chief of Defence Staff at the time, seemed unconcerned. "These are detestable murderers and scumbags, I'll tell you that right up front. They detest our freedoms, they detest our society, they detest our liberties." But discounting Canadian human rights values drove a wedge into public opinion about the war. If we were complicit with torturers, was the war worth it?

---

4. Graeme Smith, "From Canadian Custody into Cruel Hands," *The Globe and Mail*, April 23, 2007

5. Graeme Smith, "House of Pain: Canada's Connection with Kandahar's Ruthless Palace Guard," *The Globe and Mail*, April 10, 2010

6. Paul Koring, "Ottawa Kept Abuse Charges against Afghan Ally Secret," *The Globe and Mail*, February 1, 2008

After Canada's Foreign Minister, Maxime Bernier, complained to President Karzai, Assadullah was reassigned and eventually became head of Afghan intelligence. Then Karzai called an Afghan–Canadian, Tooryalai Wesa, and said, "I need you to be governor in Kandahar."

Toor was born in Kohak, an ancient village across the Argandhab River from Kandahar city. The family farm was on well-irrigated soil and grew wheat, corn, rice and cotton. The Wesa orchards contained apricot and apple trees along with grapes and plump pomegranates that yielded an exquisite ruby red juice. It was a simple and peaceful life in "the good old days" before the crosscurrents of ideological and geopolitical conflicts shredded stable traditions.

There was no school in Kohak, so when it was time for Toor to begin his education, his father took him and his cousins to Kandahar city. They went back home to the family farm on the weekends. He liked school and excelled in his studies. Because he was a farm boy and his heart was close to the family land, Toor wanted to study agricultural technology and teach better farming methods to his village. He scored top marks on the national selection exam and was accepted at the internationally recognized University of Kabul, the only university in the country.

As it touched young Toor, the rivalry between the great powers was benign. Positive, even. "It was the wisdom of the king. He wanted to have different perspectives of education from different countries." The colleges of agriculture, engineering and education were supported by the Americans. The Russians built the Polytechnic Institute. The French were in medicine and law while the Germans helped the economics and natural sciences faculties. In 1952, the Americans had built the Dahla Dam to irrigate Kandahar; in 1964 the Russians built the Salang tunnel, an engineering marvel that cut the travel time from north to south Afghanistan from seventy-two to ten hours and ensured the route was consistently passable.

Such peaceful coexistence came to an end in the 1970s. When, in 1974, Toor's scholarship to the American University of Beirut was cut short by the civil war there, he transferred to the University of Nebraska, which had an academic relationship with Afghanistan. After graduating with a master's in agricultural science in 1977, he went back home to teach at Kabul University with plans to pursue a PhD in the US. The following year, the communist People's Democratic Party of Afghanistan (PDPA) staged a coup and President Daoud Khan and the government splintered.

The bottom fell out of Toor's plans when, with Soviet backing, the PDPA purged the university. "They assumed that everybody who studied in the US would be ideologically against them. They took professors and students from homes, workplaces and the dormitory, and then they were gone." Toor led me to understand that the victims of the purge were killed. "I was stuck. There was no way to go anywhere." When the new government decreed that anyone with more than thirty acres would have their land confiscated and redistributed, the Wesas lost their family farm of generations.

Toor managed to keep working as a teacher in the agricultural college but his brothers-in-law were murdered for ideological incorrectness. One was a military officer; the other was an engineer.

After the Soviet withdrawal in 1988, President Najibullah appointed a Minister of Higher Education to fix a shattered system. Toor was appointed as the minister's chief of staff, but hung onto his teaching job, too. "I didn't know how long this minister would be in power. I didn't want to go through the whole university recruitment process again. Plus, I was getting good pay."

In his new role, Toor recruited a couple of colleagues, made his way across the country to Kandahar city and administered the University of Kabul entrance exam for the first time in years. After the exams, Toor sent his colleagues back to Kabul while he stayed in Kandahar to talk about establishing the University of Kandahar. As is the way in Afghanistan, he consulted with everybody—the governor, elders, intellectuals and other leaders. When he returned to Kabul, he pitched a plan for a new university to serve southern Afghanistan with a focus on agriculture, the lifeblood of the regional economy. The Minister of Education approved his proposal then needed somebody to be the chancellor. The Prime Minister said it should be Toor.

Toor tried to get out of it. "Thank you, but I can't do that. I have three young girls at home. My wife is a doctor. She's on call sometimes." The minister appealed to Prime Minister Fazal Haq Khaliqyar, arguing that anybody else would take extra time to get up to speed. The Prime Minister told Toor, "You started it. You have to do it." Toor knew his family would be unhappy with him but respect for authority is deeply rooted in Afghani culture. One simply cannot say no to presidents or prime ministers.

In 1990, Toor went to Kandahar despite the danger posed by the ongoing fighting, leaving his wife and daughters in Kabul for safety. He transformed an old military base into a campus for the initial class of fifteen students. Parade grounds became soccer fields, offices became classrooms and officers' quarters were converted to faculty housing.

Even though Kandahar University would offer a better future to the province's youth, the mujahideen sent in rockets twice a day—in the morning between 10:00 and 11:00 and then in the afternoon between 3:00 and 4:00. When the government fell apart and the mujahideen entered Kandahar, they took over the campus and all its land, putting their own families in the campus housing. Toor admitted defeat and went back to Kabul, now an unemployed citizen of a failing state.

Shortly after his return, in 1991, Toor's wife Rangina became ill. As the security situation was also getting worse and worse, the family left the country to seek treatment in Moscow, where Toor's brother was going to school. They were still there in April 1992 when the mujahideen ousted President Najibullah. It became too dangerous to return to Afghanistan, so Toor went to Budapest where he managed to get a job teaching agricultural extension, supplementing traditional farming practices with scientific techniques. As nobody knew if instability from the recent collapse of the Soviet Union would make his stay in Hungary untenable, he began visiting embassies using the diplomatic passport he held as a result of his role as chancellor. He finally got a visa for Switzerland and bought his family a one-way train ticket to Zurich over the objections of his children, who longed to return to their life in Kabul.

Arriving at the huge Zurich train station with no money, no Swiss friends and no place to stay, Toor told his family to wait with their bags on a bench in the train station and to stay put until he returned. He hurried to the first phone booth he could find, planning to flip through the pages on the slim chance there would be a familiar name that he could call for help. The phone booth was occupied by "a guy on the phone wearing Afghan clothes." It turned out that he was Pakistani, but his roommate, Ahmadullah, was Kandahari. Ahamadullah showed up within a half hour and took them to his room in the basement of the hospital where he worked as a labourer.

The family got through the night thanks to the generosity of a compatriot, but Toor realized that they could not live like this. The next day, Ahmadullah showed them the way to the Zurich police station. "And that was the hardest day of my life. I requested asylum and I thought, That's it. I can never go back to Afghanistan." The police sent them to the refugee receiving centre on the border with Germany where the Wesa family joined displaced Albanians, Bosnians and Kosovars.

Toor soon found his way to the Institute of Agricultural Economics at the University of Zurich. He used the library to access professional journals and introduced himself to academic peers. Six months later, the department head asked if he could help with a project in Kazakhstan. He received police permission and the family settled in Zurich. The girls were top students and happy in school but children of refugees were not eligible for Swiss university at that time so, with the eldest ready to graduate, it was time for another move.

Toor said to Rangina, "We left the country because of these three girls. If they are unable to go on to higher education, that's a crime for us. You are a medical doctor. I have a masters from the US. If our children do not become educated, I will never forgive myself." Desperate to find a country that would give his girls the academic opportunities their parents had had, Toor applied for jobs with universities across Canada and Australia. After multiple rejections, the University of British Columbia finally offered him a PhD program plus ten hours of work a week.

But first, he needed a visa. Toor and his family travelled to the Canadian Embassy in Bern to meet with a visa officer. Like all visa officers, she was empowered with the awesome authority to ask unlimited personal, financial, health and professional questions. It is a power that determines the destiny of applicants and future generations.

For bureaucrats, saying "no" is the lowest risk option, especially to a university candidate from a failed state where it is not possible to check if someone is complicit in war crimes, terrorism or opium trafficking. But sometimes the warmth of shared humanity enters the equation. After a full interview and a forty-minute wait, the visa officer asked Toor's three girls to come into her office. Before long they skipped out wearing little Canadian flags pined on their blouses. The immigration officer said, "Congratulations, you are accepted as autonomous refugees to Canada. You will be on your own."

In 1995, Toor began his studies as the first Afghan PhD student at UBC. The UBC international student centre had a world map with flags from students hailing from every continent. There was no Afghan flag, so he got one and proudly added it. Over the next twelve years, Toor completed his doctorate and published his thesis on agricultural reform in Afghanistan. He also visited Afghanistan to work on development projects with organizations including USAID and the UN's Food and Agriculture Organization. His academic career advanced until 2008, when President Karzai called with another request he could not refuse.

Before I concluded my courtesy call with Toor, we talked about Operation Hamkari and established an ambitious schedule. Every week we met in the palace conference room to discuss governance and development in a particular district, either in the countryside or in Kandahar city. The district leader would attend to tell the governor and his ministers what the community needed and what it was worried about. The KPRT would then match projects and funding to district needs to show the government was leading the delivery of international aid.

It was good, but it was not enough. Meetings of officials inside the governor's palace did not connect the government to people where they lived. To show leadership in the contested areas, Toor had to get out in the countryside and meet district leaders; it was important that he be seen as a native Kandahari and a man of the people, not as a Canadian who had been dropped into Kandahar.

To get anything done as governor, Toor had to walk a narrow path. Taking back government land from warlords was a very risky proposition, but it had to be done. Eradicating poppy fields to stem the opium revenue that financed the Taliban also had to be done. But taking on too many opponents at the same time could get a person killed.

Toor was careful to treat the Taliban with a modicum of respect, always referring to them as the opposition. And he developed a sort of modus vivendi with Ahmed Wali Karzai, the powerful Chairman of the Provincial Council able to keep the other warlords in line, partially at least. He made space for Toor to govern but it was a small space with murky boundaries that didn't stop the assassination attempts.

Toor was a target because groups on all sides were willing to kill to protect their power, money and territory. Warlords and Taliban were united in their opposition to a working government. "The opposition wanted to stop us from doing anything. They just wanted us to be confined to the palace," Toor told me. From the opposition point of view, a public assassination scares citizens and calls into question the competence and courage of the government. If they can't protect themselves, how can they protect the people?

Despite the risks, Toor knew that citizens wanted their governor to be visible and accessible. The people expected their leaders to show their faith in public, particularly on the holy day of Eid. This ancient and annual celebration of shared belief presents an excellent targeting opportunity—a public event whose time and place are fixed and known by everybody.

In 2009, the opposition placed an IED along Toor's route to the mosque. When his Land Cruiser drove past, the concealed assassin triggered the bomb, perhaps using a cell phone or garage door opener. At that close distance the explosion, the sound and the shock wave were felt simultaneously. A plume of grey smoke rose over the scene and everything was enveloped in dust.

Toor, his driver and bodyguard all survived with minor injuries from the broken glass and raced back to the safety of the palace. "I went to the palace for an hour or so," Toor said, "then went back to perform my prayers at the mosque. I stayed to let them know that we are not giving up because of a bomb. We have our own agenda. We have security and we have power."

On another occasion, there were simultaneous suicide attacks on both sides of the palace. During the assault, an American soldier was wounded and evacuated by helicopter to the hospital at KAF. A local TV reporter filed a story that Toor had escaped with him. When an outraged Toor confronted the reporter in the palace press centre, the poor journalist said the opposition had told him to lie. "I am sure it was one of those Provincial Council members or tribal leaders. There was a lot of blood on the ground and we tried to wash it, but it was not a good day."

On yet another occasion, Toor learned that an unsuccessful suicide bomber had been captured and detained by the National Directorate of Security. The director of intelligence explained that the captive had been hiding in a cemetery beside the road, waiting to become a "sucker bomb" after an IED buried on the road to Kandahar Airfield exploded. His instructions were to wait for the foreign forces to arrive. When they did, he was to run amongst them and blow himself up, killing as many as possible.

To the hapless bomber's dismay, the first responders were Afghan police; no international forces arrived. As his drugs started to wear off, he realized he had a problem. He may have been told that handlers would kill him if he failed. Or perhaps he thought his family would lose the money that they had been promised. Either way, the Taliban would never give him a way out. Scared, confused and alone, he went to a nearby house. The residents called the police to inform them of this unwelcome guest.

"I want to talk to him," said Toor.

The NDS brought the captive to Toor's office. "Did you ask your handler why he was not the one to put on an explosive vest and do the job himself?" he asked.

"I did ask him," came the reply. "He told me that, if he did it, I would never go to Paradise. If he carried out the bombing, there would be no one to recruit me. And then I would never go to Paradise."

Suicide bombings were a recent practice in Afghanistan. The mujahideen never used suicide bombers against the Soviets and the Taliban did not systematically recruit suicide bombers until they learned they would lose any conventional military offensive against combined NATO and Afghan forces. Perhaps inspired by the success of Al Qaeda suicide bombing in Iraq, the first such event recorded in Afghanistan was in 2004. The Taliban recruitment stream passed through schools of religious instruction, known as madrassas, especially in neighbouring Pakistan, where they were free from interruption by Afghan authorities or NATO soldiers.

By definition, suicide bombing needs constant renewal. It also needs an enabling social environment, one of poverty, ignorance and anger. Many grievances flowed from civilian casualties caused by pro-government forces, whether because of a bomb falling on the wrong target and killing a family or family members taken captive for interrogation and imprisonment, restoring family pride and community honour was an abundant motivator, even though about three-quarters of all civilian deaths were caused by Taliban activity.

Howard Coombs, our counterinsurgency advisor, told me that there was sometimes family support as well. They go to their death knowing that their families will be rewarded with about a hundred dollars and maybe a small parcel of land.

A twisted religious education shapes suicide bombers, often young adolescents or even children, to obey their recruiters, especially if linked with local mullahs. These religious leaders play a governance role in the community, settling disputes between landowners over boundaries (hundreds of years old, unsurveyed and scrambled by the displacement of people by conflict) or advising the correct amount of blood money to be paid to the victim's family when a fight results in a killing. In the absence of police and courts, the mullah listens to each party and conveys God's solution so that good relations between families are restored. Everyone benefits from his unquestioned authority.

When I asked Rambo about Taliban suicide bombers, he explained, "They draw pictures of heaven on the walls of the madrassas. There are streams of milk, and there are girls." Away from their families for the first time in their lives, adolescent boys are exposed to relentless grooming for death. "They've been brainwashed by fake scholars of Islam. Or real scholars, but for money."

A devout Muslim like most Afghans, Rambo was offended by this cruel manipulation of impressionable young men. With anger he said, "They are just faking Islam and persuading them with cheap tricks. Brainwashing them to go and fight for Islam. In their schools, they taught impoverished and ignorant young boys that fighting and dying for the Taliban was better than living. That they would get seventy virgins, and every pleasure conceivable to young male minds if they died fighting the Afghan government and foreigners. There's no way Islam is like that. This is a fake story that they made up to get these ignorant people to die for them."

Toor told me that, while suicide bombers weren't motivated by money, the Taliban handlers who recruited and manipulated them certainly were. They needed it to pay and arm their fighters, so they accepted commissions from clients willing to pay to get rid of political opponents or business rivals. He shared the fee scale for Taliban assassinations: US$100,000 for the highest value targets such as governors, mayors and police chiefs, less for lower-status targets including deputy governors, or district leaders.

In all, Toor survived twelve assassination attempts. The last was in 2015, four years after we had left Kandahar. The attacker approached the guard in the lobby of the governor's office and said that he had a petition to deliver. As the guard examined his papers, the attacker grabbed the guard's gun, shot him and moved to the next room. He overpowered the next guard and entered the governor's office just as Toor moved into the adjacent conference room, locking the door behind him. He heard the detonation of explosives that must have been hidden in the assassin's sandals before the American military liaison entered and shot the attacker, getting wounded in the process.

Although our mission was technically over, Phil Lupul, the political director of our team, was still in Kandahar monitoring the prison conditions of the fighters we had captured and handed over to the Afghans. Two days after the assassination attempt, Phil paid a courtesy call on the governor to say goodbye.

Phil said, "His office was all shot up and burned out. He took me around and showed me. There were bullet holes everywhere. The attacker had pounded on the door, screaming at him and shooting through the door. When I saw the governor, the office was still a wreck. But he was there, working."

It was the same office in which I had first paid my courtesy call.

# CHAPTER EIGHT

## WEAVING A BASKET OUT OF SNAKES

I came out of my chilled concrete office to get some breakfast. It felt like the desert sun had burned the oxygen out of the atmosphere as I walked across the dusty brown grass of our yard, past the latrine and shower block to the mess tent, its khaki fabric inflated by high-powered air conditioners.

One of the first things to transition to US control was the mess. I passed by the eggs, bacon, pancakes, hash browns, short-order griddle and little boxes of Frosted Flakes, Sugar Pops and other cereals.I passed a fridge of Red Bull, Monster and sodas, then grabbed a yogurt and coffee. Breakfast was almost finished and most soldiers had gone out on operations. I went to an empty table for twelve, grateful for the solitude.

An American private sat down at the other end of the table. On his tray were a couple of cans of Red Bull and about ten hardboiled eggs. He pulled off the whites, ate them and discarded the yolks. Like most of his comrades, this soldier didn't want to talk to strangers and we both ate in silence. In the buzz of air conditioners and the glare of fluorescent lights, I thought about Ahmed Wali Karzai, popularly known as AWK, the warlord I was about to visit. I had only been in Kandahar a month and was still learning to navigate the three complex circles of power.

The first circle was the power-broker world of tribes, guns, opium, money and secret prisons. In many ways, it cohabitated with the insurgency in the countryside. Real influence lived here when it came to fighting a combatant who is woven into the fabric of society, indistinguishable from young farmers and shopkeepers. Power brokers like AWK reached into tribes and villages to make things happen. The power of tribal leaders preceded and existed independently from national and provincial governments; tribes were represented by the Provincial Council.

The second circle was the government of the Islamic Republic of Afghanistan. Created at the Bonn conference, negotiated by Afghans and shaped by Western governments, it hovered lightly over traditional Afghanistan like an organization chart printed on a transparency. It had a modern constitution and a structure of ministries and provinces with an elected president, Hamid Karzai, who appointed the governors of the provinces and districts. His mandate was to extend security, governance and development across the full territory of Afghanistan—a mandate that ran counter to provincial councils full of warlords.

The third circle was the international one, dominated by the United States, where military might and economic power were deployed simultaneously to achieve strategic objectives. We believed that when NATO and the Afghan forces drove the Taliban out of populated lands, a democratic Afghan government would take root.

Back in my office, I proceeded to the waist-high two-by-four cross that held my protective gear and got ready to leave the base. First came my flak jacket with the Kevlar body armour. Over that came the tactical vest, essential equipment in the pockets: flameproof gloves (if an IED explodes under your vehicle, or your helicopter crashes, the doors are burning hot) and knife (to cut your way out if your seatbelt is stuck). Last came my ballistic glasses with three shades of lenses (dark green for day, clear for night and yellow for cloudy days). At an early safety training session, we were shown a used pair with a razor-sharp piece of shrapnel sticking out of one lens. Everybody wore their ballistic glasses.

Ty was waiting at the door. Today, my Deputy Political Director, Greg Galligan, would also be accompanying us. At thirty, Greg was among the more experienced members of the team, having served in Tel Aviv. Greg's Irish heritage comes through in his thick curly black hair and bright blue eyes. A self-described "pretty chill guy," he's a good talker and a quick thinker.

Like many in the early stages of a diplomatic career, he wanted to test himself and to prove his value to the Department of Foreign Affairs. He also knew that, five years into the mission, the pool of candidates willing to go to Kandahar had been depleted. "I had been to Gaza. I had been to the West Bank. Afghanistan was the big issue in government at that time and I thought I understood the whole idea of moving from counterterrorism to counterinsurgency." Greg brought energy, curiosity and an incisive mind to the team. He also brought a winning sense of fun that leavened the heavy setting. He could be deadly serious when necessary but he could also share a few laughs.

We would go in our usual convoy, a dozen or so soldiers in three armoured vehicles painted to match the Dijon-mustard yellow of Kandahar dust. Ty, Greg and I walked to the assembly point for Orders while the vehicles idled patiently. The last twenty-four hours had not seen any attacks on our planned path across the city, nor had new information on threats been intercepted.

We entered the LAV through the back and strapped into our four-point seatbelts, then watched the city pass by through bullet-proof portholes. Little boys splashed and laughed in the irrigation ditches. Little girls in school uniforms skipped brightly on their way to classrooms that Canada had built. Women in black or sky-blue burkas carried brightly coloured shopping bags. Chaotic swarms of Indian motorized tricycles and cheap Chinese motorcycles dodged around and past our four-wheeled behemoth with daring uncon-cern. Snub-nosed Bedford jingle trucks lovingly adorned with shiny tin pendants, silky window fringes and intricate paintings on every square inch, nonchalantly shared the road with us, their exhaust as loud as their colours. Somehow a little of that carefree happiness penetrated the steel armour surrounding us and lifted our hearts.

Our route took us past the central cemetery, a dusty field of serenity with scattered knots of mourners. Sometimes a few small concrete blocks marked the border of a grave, or a flat stone had been placed upright. Other times a simple plaque displayed a few words in Arabic script. The modesty of the graves expressed the humility and equality with which the faithful are expected to depart this transitory life.

Dig down two thousand years and the prayers for the departed are in Greek. I thought about the millennia of civilizational strata below us and hoped that our mark would be inscribed on the good side of history's ledger.

When we arrived at our destination, the soldiers dismounted and moved in patrol formation to secure a path for our entry. Invisible to us, Strike Force—AWK's personal militia and security company—would have established a deeper level of perimeter protection. Once the soldiers were in place, the three of us waded through a sea of humble supplicants milling about, trying to find a way past the gatekeepers.

People came to AWK for many reasons. Perhaps they wanted part of a lucrative NATO contract or a son-in-law needed a government job. A land dispute may have escalated into a tribal conflict he would have to settle. He was known for helping people get to India for medical treatment unavailable in Afghanistan. There might be Taliban movements he needed to know about.

AWK was the ultimate address for political messages in Kandahar because he had secured benefits from all three circles of power. The Afghan president, Hamid Karzai, was his half-brother. As a member of an influential Kandahari family, he had his finger on the pulse of every village and tribal leader. The influential Popalzai tribe recognized him as their chief and he had been selected as chairman of the Provincial Council. Plus, he was said to have a close working relationship with the CIA.

There were numerous media allegations that he was vastly

corrupt, had associations with the billion-dollar heroin trade and colluded with the Taliban. Congressional committees had talked about him. Many diplomats and military leaders believed that AWK and others like him were "malign actors" and that replacing them with ethical leaders was the only path to stability and progress for Afghanistan. My predecessor, Ben Rowswell, was one of them.

When he arrived in Kandahar, Ben soon saw that Canada required an independent understanding of the political leaders with whom we were working. So, risky as it was, he sent Canadian political officers outside the wire to find out what ordinary Afghans thought about AWK. "We were trying to understand the base reality. They were furious with AWK's abuses of power," he said. "He ran secret prisons for his business adversaries. If someone didn't pay up on a contract or crossed him, he would throw them into a basement of one of his residences and hold him there. I never saw any hard evidence, but there were widespread rumours that he was heavily involved in selling opium."

A confidential US Embassy report from a meeting Ben attended later leaked during the Wikileaks scandal: "While we must deal with AWK as the head of the Provincial Council, he is widely understood to be corrupt and a narcotics trafficker." Ben tried his very best to find a way to diminish the influence of AWK but, just before I got there to replace him, the top NATO commander in the region and the senior American civilian told Ben to "call off your dogs." Another senior American said, "We're here to defeat terrorists and he is very good at fighting terrorists. So we're with him." As a result, AWK remained the most powerful man in Kandahar.

As we made our way into AWK's compound, I hoped there would be no press coverage or photos of me with him. Inside, we passed men crowding the lobby and lining up on the stairs to his receiving rooms. Except for people like us, Kandahar is not a city of appointments.

We were seated at a long and ornate dining table covered with a white cloth. Glass cupboards filled with fine china surrounded us. A servant poured tea.

AWK occupied the cultures of North America and Afghanistan simultaneously and completely. When the communists took control in 1979, the Karzai family pulled him out of high school to join the millions of their countrymen in the diaspora. But instead of refugee camps in Iran and Pakistan, they found their way to Chicago and obtained green cards.

As with many newcomers to the US and Canada, the restaurant business beckoned. The Karzai family called their restaurant Helmand, after the river shared by Afghanistan and Iran. Framed antique pictures of old Afghanistan and uniformed waiters in black jackets and white shirts gave it an authentic feel, and the cuisine was inviting. Afghan food is warm and gentle in flavour and texture. Lamb, beef and chicken are cooked patiently for a mouthfeel that comforts. Spicing is soft. Aromas of cinnamon, clove and cumin float over the fluffy rice that accompanies stews and charcoal-grilled meats.

Under AWK's management, the Helmand was successful and profitable. A sports fan, he became an ardent supporter of the Chicago Cubs. In the late nineties, when he left Chicago to go help his father in Pakistan, AWK sold the business to Jack Jones, who replaced the Helmand with Jack's on Halsted. Jack said of AWK, "He was a classy gentleman to do business with and he cared about us. He cared about what we were going to do here, that we were going to be successful and everything was going to be okay."[7]

Today, AWK wore an Afghan vest over a white button-down shirt that covered a well-fed paunch. Heavy five o'clock shadow darkened a light complexion that suggested an interior and nocturnal life. A droopy moustache separated fleshy lips from a big nose. He did not wear a turban as an elder would, or even the jaunty

---

7. Natalie Martinez, "Slain Half-Brother of Afghan President Ran Chicago Resto," NBC Chicago (blog), July 13, 2011, https://www.nbcchicago.com/news/local/ahmed-wali-karzai-chicago/1905924/. Accessed February, 2024

Pashtun cap favoured by younger Kandaharis. His hand was clean, soft and dry when I shook it. We were both six feet tall and he met my gaze directly, his dark eyes serious and sad.

We sat down across from each other. He did not bring note-takers or translators. Greg would write our report to ensure Ottawa knew exactly what was said.

Friendly, businesslike and calm, he spoke fluent American English with hints of a soft midwestern accent that blended pleasingly with the courteous and deliberate Afghan manner of speaking. He could have been one of us. There were pleasantries, but neither of us had time to waste by prolonging them. I only had two things to say and he had a house full of anxious supplicants.

"I came to talk to you about the parliamentary elections," I began. He knew this and nodded, listening carefully. "Canada expects the elections to be free and fair. It's important to the government and people of Canada that the elections are clean. Our continued support depends on governance we can respect."

Canada and other NATO countries had poured millions into building democratic institutions and training Afghan electoral officials in advance of national elections scheduled for September 18. To our way of thinking, and for millions of progressive Afghans, letting the people choose their leaders through free and fair elections was the right way to run a country. Democracy would empower the good guys; dirty elections might puncture support for the mission at home. A new parliament held promise for social change, too. Sixty-eight seats were reserved for women and separate female polling stations had been established. The KPRT was financing democracy projects such as the Afghan Women & Children Rights Protection Association established to teach civic education to women.

The big question was security at the polling stations. The Taliban had issued a blanket threat. "Everything and everyone affiliated with the election is our target—candidates, security forces, campaigners, election workers, voters are all our targets." Candidates and their families were fired on. President Karzai's cousin was running for a seat and narrowly missed being killed by a Taliban IED attack. Four of his bodyguards were killed and three were wounded.

Across the province, there would be 538 polling stations for males, 306 stations for females, and thirty-nine stations for the nomadic Kuchi people. Canadian forces would partner with the Afghan army and show a presence in key locations, while maintaining a respectful distance so as not to spook nervous voters or make the polls more of a Taliban target. In a meeting with us at the KPRT, the Electoral Complaints commissioners said that they were not optimistic about being able to investigate or prevent fraud.

AWK nodded. We both knew he was in a position to determine the outcome of the elections, probably already had. He had previously engineered widespread, very visible fraud, stealing the 2009 election for his half-brother, Hamid Karzai, in a way that flagrantly undermined the international mission. My underlying message was for him to know that we cared and to ensure he factored our interests into his choices.

He said what he had to say. "The elections will not be interfered with. There will be no problem."

Sitting at his dining room table, I was conflicted about how to deal with AWK. I had to be clear with him, but I couldn't push too hard. He was the brother of President Karzai and I needed a relationship with him to be effective as RoCK. Diplomatic disrespect would insult him and shut off my access, damaging my credibility and the team's effectiveness. If AWK and his brother the president were getting money from the CIA, my diplomatic influence would be marginal anyway. Money speaks louder than words. I decided to be clear and cordial to keep the Canadian channel open.

I turned to a more congenial topic. To support institutions of government in Kandahar, Canada was replacing the Provincial Council building blown up in 2009. The attack was an early demonstration of the Taliban brand of spectacular violence. First, a car bomb was crashed into the entry gates and detonated. Through the smoke and panic, three fighters disguised in Afghan army uniforms ran in as if to rescue, then sprayed machine gun fire everywhere. When the real Afghan police responded, the fighters detonated their explosive vests. Thirteen people were killed.

AWK had left the building less than an hour earlier, having attended a governance seminar conducted by the National Democratic Institute of the United States. It was one of the nine assassination attempts on him. Maybe that explained some of the sadness in his hooded eyes.

I said, "The new Provincial Council building is a visible expression of democracy that should be given profile. I'll be there and it will be important for you to be there."

AWK had been personally involved in the design of the building. "Yes. It's gonna be beautiful. I'll be there too. Let's talk about timing closer to the day."

The election issue and opening of the Provincial Council building dealt with, AWK turned to what was existential—Operation Medusa. "If it wasn't for the Canadians, we would have lost to the Taliban four years ago." He owed his life to Canada and was sincerely grateful. There was an involuntary rise in the register of his soft voice. "We didn't know if we would survive."

The Taliban did not keep people like AWK prisoner. They would have killed him, and probably in a spectacular fashion, to broadcast a message of terror. Clear in his mind would have been the fate of the ex-president, Mohammad Najibullah. The first time the Taliban took power in 1996, it was reported that they entered the UN compound where the then president had been under protection, took him away, tortured, shot and castrated him and hung his bloated body in a main square.

After bidding us a polite farewell, AWK returned to his receiving room packed with tribal elders in robes and turbans waiting for him to render judgements or distribute largess.

On voting day, Governor Wesa took the mayor and thirty journalists to watch him vote. On the way, his convoy was hit by a roadside bomb. He shook it off and continued to the polling centre.

In other countries, I would have been there with an election observation team, as is standard practice for Canada in democratizing countries. The routine is to assess conditions for a free and fair vote, including risks of voter intimidation, in advance. On election days, observers drop unannounced into multiple polling stations to see if voters can mark and cast their ballot in secrecy, and if election workers safely store ballots and keep them free from tampering. At the close of polls, observers watch the count, along with local scrutineers.

In Kandahar, it was too dangerous for international observers to monitor the election directly, so the KPRT political officers made constant calls to check in with civil society organizations, the Electoral Commission and candidates.

Expectations for rural voter turnout were low. In the prior year's presidential elections, only fifteen to twenty percent of registered voters felt motivated or secure enough to cast their ballot. We thought a better turnout this time would signal that improved security made Kandaharis more willing to vote.

The elections were disappointing. Expanded numbers of NATO and Afghan forces in Kandahar did not result in significantly better participation. Only one in five Kandaharis cast their ballot. There were reports of a village leader using multiple voter cards to stuff ballot boxes. The women's vote was compromised. Some female polling centres were specifically targeted for fraud. Many women showed up to vote but left without casting their ballot because of a lack of female searchers available to ensure they were not armed.

Even so, we assessed it as marginally better than the 2009 presidential election. Countries supporting Afghanistan, like Canada, congratulated the Afghan people.

As promised, AWK attended the opening of the new Provincial Council building. It was graced by arches, inlays of beautiful Helmand marble, Kunar wood and fine carpets. Like many public buildings in Kandahar, the landscaping of flowering trees and shrubs was delightful.

Democracy in Afghanistan did not have a fertile field in which to grow. Canadian efforts were sincere, but elections were not creating democracy. The warlord political culture was just too strong. Kandaharis told us they had been disappointed by the performance of their elected representatives, who were more interested in pursuing personal interests than the well-being of their constituents, and warlords like AWK had no interest in squandering hard-won power in fair-minded contests. Many Kandaharis had developed a cynical and pessimistic attitude toward elections.

As I stood beside AWK, I came to a bitter realization that when Kandaharis saw me and others cutting ribbons and announcing contributions, they saw power alignment, not democracy, much less government legitimacy. But good guys don't come first in failed states like Afghanistan and we were in no position to hold auditions for preferred power brokers. Building governance in that place was like weaving a basket out of snakes.

# CHAPTER NINE

## DARE TO KNOW

I looked forward to evenings, when the tempo of work tended to settle and I could finally close my three computers. Around 8:00 p.m., Major Attenborough[8] would step in, close the door behind him and take a seat in one of the overstuffed armchairs across from my desk. I would come around and take the other.

Major Attenborough was a member of All-Source Intelligence Centre (ASIC). The team was based at KAF, but we had a satellite office in Camp Nathan Smith, ASIC Forward, for KPRT intelligence needs. The major handed me a file of reports, each on sky-blue paper. A list of people who had seen them was recorded in an accompanying register. The sensitivity of this material was such that Major Attenborough was supposed to be present any time they were out of secure storage.

The position of RoCK required me to have a Top-Secret clearance for Canada and a COSMIC Top Secret for NATO. The top-secret classification meant that these documents and the information they contained would cause grave damage to Canada if exposed or in the wrong hands. If I were to accidentally leave a confidential report on my desk, mixed up with the flurry of reports and memos on white paper, the security guard who prowled our halls as we slept would take it and leave in its place an infraction notice. Three infractions would get me cut off and would be very embarrassing.

The major handed me the one on top. "You will want to see this one, Tim."

8. Not his real name

There were indications of a secret prison where a warlord was locking up his enemies or competitors, a common and effective method of intimidation. I would have to follow up to make sure it didn't touch on Canadian-captured detainees. "Can I get an assessment of the meaning and reliability of this intel?"

"Sure. We'll get right on it."

I went through the rest of the reports. Some confirmed what I already knew. Some were fresh. All included information we could not collect overtly.

"Let's go over the RoCK information requirements," I said. ASIC Forward's priorities were based on my intelligence priorities, without which the mass of information would be overwhelming.

"Here they are." He showed me a list of what his team was working on.

"Keep a focus on prisoner treatment and add a lookout for any sign of peace negotiations and contact with the Taliban, especially in Panjwai," I said. There had been talk of a demobilization process in the future, though things were pretty sketchy at this point. I fervently hoped it would happen. Maybe it could lead to a peace process and an end to the war. "Thanks, Major. That was a really good package."

"A lot of monkey business going on out there," he chuckled, putting the file of papers in his satchel. "See you tomorrow."

The ASIC shoulder patch depicts a brown squirrel holding a precious silver acorn under a Canadian maple leaf. Like squirrels, ASIC collected intelligence from all over the place: open sources like Kandahari TV and radio, intelligence reports shared by allies, intercepted cell phone conversations and interviews with insiders and diplomats.

Coming in as we did for only one year, without training in the Pashtun culture or language, and with little knowledge of Afghanistan's obscure history, it was difficult but essential to figure out what the hell was going on, who the hell we were working with and who we were fighting. We needed to know who was making decisions, and who was influencing communities and their leaders.

Who received big contracts from Western countries was a good indicator of power, money and alignment. So was observing who the Taliban were trying to eliminate through their campaign of intimidation, and who they decided to leave alone. A telephone intercept might expose a local businessman negotiating a payment with a Taliban commander to ensure safe transport for his merchandise through Taliban territory. A two-page analysis could explain the intentions of a government leader, and how he planned to navigate clan conflicts or confront the opium trade. Sometimes intelligence is best consumed raw: that is, the transcript of exactly what was said by persons of interest. Collected in Pashtu, it was translated into English.

Sometimes the clues were indirect, like the pattern of life. Are people moving around freely? Where are they going? If one day the farmers stay home instead of tilling their fields, were they told by the Taliban to keep out of that particular area because of a planned military operation? Did they know something was going to happen? The ASIC team looked at situations through different prisms, so we could enhance our overall awareness and understanding of Kandahar.

The chief of political intelligence for ASIC was Collin Goodlet. Based in the Task Force Kandahar headquarters at KAF, he and his colleagues from Canadian forces, Foreign Affairs and Canadian intelligence services worked out of an expedient, immediate and transitory building: two layers of modified shipping containers with external stairs that sat on top of each other like grey/beige Legos. Inside was a room with the special gear and the insulated walls required to handle secret information and protect it from the prying eyes and devices of others. Collin's team also included Americans whose ability to collect intelligence through multiple methods is unsurpassed. His team's objective was white situational awareness—information about the civilian government in Kandahar and the constellation of tribal leaders, power brokers and Afghan officials whose behaviour and choices affected our mission. Red intelligence focused on the enemy, the Taliban in our case. Blue was for allies outside the extensive and tight intelligence-sharing relationship we enjoyed with our Five Eyes partners: the intelligence alliance with the US, UK, Australia and New Zealand.

Collin was one of those rare people who could be friendly and cheerful while working on the most dark and disturbing issues. Tall, he moves with loose-limbed athleticism. His droll sense of humour rests comfortably on a foundation of firm self-possession. He and other members of his team had been recruited for their intellectual and analytical capabilities through a special Canadian government program developed to find the smartest young Canadians in graduate schools around the world and attract them to public service.

Collin's first degree was in psychology, and that interest was a primary driver: he wanted to understand what motivates people to go to war. Having grown up in Canada, Collin had never experienced the enormity of full-blown war. In Afghanistan, deadly conflict was normal and had been for generations. He wanted to know what that was like. "Though we normalize it and even romanticize it, for a person to have orders to kill other people and do it with the backing of a nation-state is an extreme and risky form of behaviour. It requires people to set aside the morals their parents taught them and adopt new forms of ethics and conduct. And then it requires soldiers to set those extreme behaviours aside again in peacetime. Whether it is taking out those who are planting IEDs to protect your comrades, or an offensive operation to clear a village of the Taliban, it's extreme even if you are convinced the cause is just."

Intelligence officers strive to provide hard and cold analysis uncoloured by fuzzy values or policy advocacy. But people are complex, especially when the absence of legitimate governance leads to alternate sources of power. It could take Collin's team a week to sift through multiple sources of intelligence, some of it contradictory, to identify tribal allegiances, clan affiliations, commercial interests, religious authority, historic family grievances, territorial or water disputes and other factors to determine who we could trust and who was likely playing a double game. It is a kind of analysis that demands mental acrobatics and razor-sharp thinking. Forming alliances or attacking targets without understanding the first, second and third-order effects could lead to unintended and undesirable consequences.

The ASIC intelligence delivered by Major Attenborough was vital and provided us with the essential facts and analysis necessary to navigate the puzzle of Kandahar. It gave us a way to assess what we were being told and made the pitfalls and bear traps out there visible before we stepped on them. Gathered from within KAF, it was critical to the safety of personnel operating outside the wire. Conversely, reports from the field supplemented ASIC's intelligence.

Understanding Kandahari culture and its hidden structures of power from the field was one responsibility of Bernard Haven. A development economist trained at the London School of Economics, Bernard was originally posted at KAF, where he coordinated civilian and military policies. After moving to the KPRT as a Senior Development Officer, he visited remote towns and villages to see what was happening with development projects, a good indicator of how the campaign was going.

Bernard was working in Nigeria with CIDA when NATO asked Canada to provide a development expert to work on projects in RC South with colleagues from the UK (in Helmand province) and the Netherlands (in Uruzgan and Daikudi). Attracted by the adventure and excitement of contributing to the largest international security priority in the world, Bernard applied.

Bernard did not have extensive experience in conflict zones, didn't speak that language and was still trying to navigate the fluid, confusing and elaborate multinational military environment but, at twenty-six, he "quickly realized when you go out to the districts that you are a wise old soul here with these eighteen-year-old soldiers who also have no idea what to do."

In early 2010, Bernard and his colleagues were putting plans together for the coming surge of both soldiers and aid. They travelled to Maiwand district by helicopter and then went on foot to check out agricultural projects. The soldiers escorting them, proud of their projects said, "Look how safe it is."

But, when he was inspecting a project, his escort said, "While you're looking, please just kneel down. You're a very large target standing up." Bernard didn't get a feeling of safety. He said to himself, "Holy smokes! I hope I don't get shot here."

The same planning group later drove down the river valley to Zhari. Because they lingered at the district centre for "a last look around," the police convoy that was to lead them back to KAF was some distance ahead. It detonated an IED buried in the road. Bernard's vehicle drove into a field to get around the danger and watched the firefight unfold through the video camera attached to the main gun on their LAV. After the Afghan police routed the Taliban, they continued back to KAF.

Bernard also accompanied the British Commander of RC South, Major General Nick Carter, to assess conditions for reconstruction in the neighbouring province of Helmand. When the helicopter landed in Sangin, buglers were on hand to welcome their commander with his regimental reveille. The twenty-first-century armour, weapons, and technology of the soldiers contrasted with the dusty agrarian reality of life in this contested district. The surge of troops in Helmand preceded a similar initiative in Kandahar, so drawing experience from the counterinsurgency campaign here would help to inform Canada's mission, with intelligence relayed through ASIC.

When Collin Goodlet's ASIC team played ball hockey against soldiers of other units and countries, they wore T-shirts that read "Dare to Know." It takes daring to obtain intelligence and report hard truths and unwelcome facts. Unlike geographical terrain, which can be captured with precision through aerial and satellite imagery, the human terrain is alien, complex and elusive. The diligence, commitment and integrity required to interpret it is reflected in the ASIC challenge coin. A tradition that dates back to the Roman legions, challenge coins are designed with symbols and slogans that express the pride of a particular military, police or intelligence organization. The ASIC challenge coin is silver. Under the image of an arctic wolf with a blood-red scar over his right eye is the motto, "Leading the Hunt."

# CHAPTER TEN

# THE CANADIAN UMBRELLA

After a visit to the Zhari district to investigate funding a camp for displaced people, I hopped on a Black Hawk helicopter to return to Camp Nathan Smith. In the back, on the floor in front of his seated captors, was a detainee being brought in for questioning at KAF. Young, scruffy and dirty, he wore a ragged brown polyester salwar kameez and flip-flops. He tried to sit up on the metal floor but couldn't help slouching to the side. His wrists were bound by a black plastic zip tie and his eyes were covered by blacked-out goggles. Over his ears were black ear protectors, like those a jack-hammer operator would wear. There was a puddle of vomit beside him. I thought he was quivering with terror, but that might have been the vibrations of the aircraft.

His captors were special forces, maybe Canadian, maybe American. I couldn't tell because they wore technical climbing clothes, the kind you might buy in a high-end outdoor store. If he were our detainee, he would be taken to a special holding facility in the Canadian Task Force area of KAF and placed in a basic cell made of chain link fencing. He would be treated according to international standards, receiving food, water and, if necessary, medical treatment while the Military Police assembled a file of the evidence related to his offence. That could range from explosive residue on his hands or clothing, possession of a weapon or having been seen planting a roadside bomb.

If the Military Police of Task Force Kandahar judged that the evidence against the detainee was insufficient for charges to be laid by the Afghans, or that he had been detained in error, they could recommend to the commander that the detainee be released. His community would be informed and asked to send an elder to fetch the liberated prisoner. A special room with Afghan carpets and appropriate furnishings had been prepared for just this purpose. Respectfully, the freed detainee would be released to the elder with the solemn explanation that this was a mistake, and the former detainee was not our enemy. The purpose of this ceremonial transfer was to restore the individual's dignity and eliminate any stain of suspicion of Taliban collusion that could interfere with reintegration into the former detainee's home community.

If, however, there was evidence against him, and the detainee was assessed as posing a threat to the Canadian forces, he and the file against him would be turned over to the National Directorate of Security (NDS), the Afghan intelligence organization established in the wake of the Taliban defeat. If charges were brought, he would be put in Sarpoza prison to await trial. Until that happened, monitoring his treatment and ensuring that no torture took place was my responsibility. The issue was politically radioactive—at the end of 2009, Prime Minister Stephen Harper had shut down parliament for three months, a move opposition parties maintained was to disrupt a parliamentary committee inquiring into the torture of Afghan detainees.

When Canada first began its mission in Kandahar in 2005, it had prepared for stabilization and reconstruction. The transformation into a vicious counterinsurgency in the summer of 2006 was a surprise, one consequence of which was that nobody in the Canadian forces or government had put in place a rights-based plan for detainees. With the army stretched to the limit and taking casualties, the expedient solution was to hand prisoners over to the new Afghan government. So that is what we did.

Others did it differently. The Dutch and the British, operating in the neighbouring provinces of Uruzgan and Helmand respectively, put in safeguards against mistreatment. But the Canadian government didn't take the problem seriously until explosive investigative reporting by *The Globe and Mail*'s Graeme Smith made the treatment of detainees front-page news. His story, published in April 2007, documented both the respectful treatment captured combatants received from their Canadian captors and the torture they faced once they were turned over to the Afghans.[9]

The systematic use of torture was one of many egregious violations of human rights suffered by Afghans in the decades preceding the Canadian mission. The Islamic Emirate of Afghanistan tortured prisoners. So did the Northern Alliance, who fought a bloody civil war against the Taliban. Retribution against enemies and revenge for transgressions was widely seen as acceptable. For warlords, many of whom operated private and illegal prisons, torture offered the combined benefits of intelligence gathering, punishment and deterrence.

Knowingly transferring prisoners into an environment where torture was commonplace was harming our national self-image and international reputation, especially against the backdrop of the "enhanced interrogation techniques" the US had sanctioned as part of its Global War on Terrorism and the shameful images of American soldiers abusing and humiliating Iraqi detainees in Abu Ghraib prison released two years previously. Some Canadian experts worried that it also constituted a war crime, a violation of our obligations as a signatory to the Geneva Conventions.

The British Columbia Civil Liberties Association and Amnesty International filed complaints with the Military Police Complaints Commission (MPCC), a civilian, quasi-judicial body. It struck a Special Parliamentary Committee on Afghanistan that, as part of its proceedings, subpoenaed the Political Director of the KPRT, Richard Colvin. As the Canadian official closest to the issues of

---

9. Graeme Smith, "From Canadian custody into cruel hands," *The Globe and Mail*, April 23, 2007

human rights and reports of torture in Kandahar, it was his job to know these things.

I had met Richard in the field during my reconnaissance mission with START in 2006. Tall, slim, with brown hair, Richard was a senior political officer and a seasoned, serious diplomat in mid-career, part of the sub-species of Canadian diplomats involved in negotiating international security and defence relations. After joining the Department of Foreign Affairs and International Trade in 1994, Richard had been posted to Sri Lanka, Russia and the Palestinian Territories.

Coming out of a painful breakup, Richard applied to go to Afghanistan in 2005 and was given two options: Political Director in the embassy in Kabul, or Political Director at the KPRT. Before making his choice, he wanted to talk to the incumbent, Glyn Berry, who was slated to be replaced in the summer of 2006. He scheduled a call with Glyn, then went on a snowboarding vacation with his brother. On January 15, Richard was sipping a coffee in a Whistler café when an image of a smoking G-Wagon flashed on the screen— it was the attack that killed Glyn.

Richard said he would help by going to Kandahar to take on Glyn's job for a couple of months until a full-time candidate could be found. Then he would go on to Kabul. In April 2006, he sat down in the office that had been Glyn's, where nothing had been touched or changed. Glyn's pictures were still on the wall; his unfinished reports were on the desk. "Glyn's death felt visceral," he said.

Richard felt psychologically prepared for what Kandahar was going to be like. His former father-in-law had fought as a Russian paratrooper in Afghanistan for two years, including in Kandahar. "I had a very good sense from him, and other Russian vets, of what we would potentially be in for, how easily it could go wrong and how careful we had to be." He also had a crystal-clear understanding of geopolitical realities. "I am not very shockable at all," he told me. But what he saw in Kandahar shocked him.

Early on, the guards called Richard to the Camp Nathan Smith gate. There was someone who wanted to talk to a Canadian: a woman, poor and evidently in distress, with three little kids. One was a baby who looked quite sick.

"Did your soldiers capture my husband?" she asked Richard through his interpreter. Her husband was a taxi driver who had gone out to work a few days ago and never returned.

Richard wanted to help. "I don't know, but I'll find out." He wrote down the husband's name, his village and the date he went missing.

He reached out to his contact in the Canadian commanding general's office and provided the information. "Could you ask the military if they detained this person?"

A day later the answer came back: "We don't know." He pressed, but the same answer came back. "We don't know."

How the fuck could they not know?

When the detainee issue blew up in Canada, Richard was in Kabul, busy on multiple files including encouraging the Afghans to beef up their forces in the south to relieve the hard-pressed Canadian troops, investigating the narcotics trade and reforming the Afghan police. Called before the Military Police Complaints Commission, Richard faced an agonizing dilemma. He believed many of the detainees being handed over were local farmers, not high-value targets, and that their treatment, in combination with aggressive counterterrorist tactics and the use of weapons such as long-range artillery, was creating fresh grievances that fueled the insurgency. He was also concerned that Canada might be violating treaties forbidding the torture of prisoners. But if he disclosed everything he knew in a public hearing, he could be accused of sharing information classified as confidential, a formal designation used to protect Canadian interests.

As he was preparing to obey the subpoena, Canada's Department of Justice warned him that he risked prosecution for revealing sensitive information. This is what Richard told Parliament: "If I refused to cooperate with the MPCC subpoena, I could be jailed for up to six months; however, if I did cooperate, under section 38 I could be jailed for up to five years."

True to his convictions, Richard testified, telling the Special Parliamentary Committee on Afghanistan that:

"During those crucial first days (after transfer by the Canadian Forces to the Afghanistan intelligence service), what happened to our detainees? According to a number of reliable sources, they were tortured. The most common forms of torture were beating, whipping with power cables, and the use of electricity. Also common was sleep deprivation, use of temperature extremes, use of knives and open flames, and sexual abuse—that is, rape. Torture might be limited to the first days or it could go on for months. According to our information, the likelihood is that all the Afghans we handed over were tortured. For interrogators in Kandahar, it was standard operating procedure."

Richard was pilloried by the Conservative government, which impugned his credibility by saying he was duped by the Taliban into thinking mistreatment occurred. It was a ridiculous and unsupportable charge.

The larger issue was the potential chill this put on diplomatic reporting. The ethic of Canadian diplomacy is to never lie. The Canadian government simply must have the unvarnished truth as observed and interpreted by its diplomatic service. A group of ex-ambassadors signed an open letter about the situation saying: "The Colvin affair risks creating a climate in which officers may be more inclined to report what they believe headquarters wants to hear, rather than facts and perceptions deemed unpalatable."

I don't know why, but the Department of Justice decided not to pursue a case against Richard.

I made sure every Afghan official I met in the prison, intelligence and police services understood there was no room for failure in preventing the torture of Canadian detainees, and that compliance was a necessary condition for our continuing support. They didn't like it, but they understood it.

To ensure compliance, Canadian political officers were assigned to interview prisoners in private to make sure they were not suffering any mistreatment and were getting the things they had a right to including fresh air, showers and the ability to worship. Monitoring was always done jointly with experts from the KPRT's Correctional Service Canada team who knew and understood international standards for prisoner treatment and prison conditions.

Political Officer Mike Detroit[10] was one of our monitors. Raised in Quebec, Mike is tough-minded and blunt-speaking, with a background in conflict studies and medieval history. Stocky, with unruly curly brown hair, he runs exactly counter to the pinstripe suit, country club stereotype often applied to diplomats. Like many of my team, he came for the adrenaline and the excitement. Sitting at a desk, or in a backwater embassy, was not for him.

The monitors were not popular with Afghan officials, who were angry about the Colvin testimony and the damage it had done to the Afghan reputation. Their cooperation always felt reluctant but that didn't matter, as long as they gave us what we needed.

In the early days of the program, a young foreign service officer went to the NDS and was told he could not visit the detainees. As acting Political Director, Mike insisted he be given access. When the head of the NDS in Kandahar refused, Mike remained in the NDS Kandahar headquarters until the head of NDS in Kabul was alerted. He told Canada to "get stuffed." No access. This was a blatant violation of the 2007 bilateral agreement with Canada that guaranteed "full and unrestricted access" by Canadian officials to detainees in Afghan custody. "You can just imagine the shit show that ensued." Ultimately, the Afghans were forced to back down.

---

10. Not his real name

"That kind of thing happened a few times. One of the head interrogators told me, 'This is really annoying because not only the Canadian detainees but all the detainees feel that there's some sort of umbrella protecting them. Because of you, we don't scare them as much, which is not good for us.'"

We could never really be sure that torture was not in fact taking place. There were reports that it continued. To ensure we had the access we needed to monitor our detainees, or to express concern about a particular case, I occasionally visited the NDS headquarters, a kind of spooky villa that had been turned into a prison, to meet with the head of NDS Kandahar, Mohammad Naeem Momeen. A general, he dressed in civilian clothes. I often saw him in a black robe and turban, with a black beard that had not started to grey. He looked well-fed and strong, and unhappy to see me. Our relationship was purely business.

Our system usually worked well. Kandaharis, almost all of whom had some kind of personal connection to detainees and prisoners, liked the Canadian umbrella, and it was useful for the US and other allies to know that Canada was going into the prisons almost every day to make sure the standards of treatment were acceptable.

"I think most detainees were happy to see us," said Mike. "There were one or two instances of detainees just being rude, but those who didn't like us just did not speak and gave us a hard look. I never had a detainee try to lay a hand on me or spit on me." A female monitor told me one of the detainees "just could not stop giggling. He had never been so close to a woman outside his family without a burka before."

According to Mike, "Eventually, it just really became routine. We had a script. You have the same conversation with the officials. They bring the detainees. We asked the questions that we were told to ask, came back and wrote our report."

My job was to read and sign off on those reports. If there were indications of mistreatment, we would go through a process of diplomatic escalation up to a formal démarche, the in-person delivery of a diplomatic note to the Foreign Ministry. A démarche constitutes an official communication from one state to the other and cannot be ignored. The process of escalating diplomatic representations to Afghan authorities took place in Kabul instead of Kandahar because it was of critical importance to conceal the detainee's identity from local authorities, who knew perfectly well who we interviewed and when.

Over the course of its mission, Canadian forces captured and transferred over a thousand detainees, though there are no reliable statistics. While there was never an allegation that Canada mistreated Afghan captives, transferring captives to Afghan authorities who had been known to use torture eroded our moral authority. When I was there, we did our best to enforce a systematic and humane approach to detain, hold and transfer detainees.

Canada's international reputation belongs to all Canadians. What the Government of Canada does overseas, it does in the name of all Canadians. As a Canadian diplomat, I'm proud of Richard Colvin's courage to speak out about torture in Kandahar. I'm proud that, as a result of controversy and shame at home, we found a practical and workable approach to improve prison conditions and protect human rights in the middle of a war. For me, it lifted a stain from our reputation.

# Chapter Eleven

# Illuminating a Black Hole

I sat in the Canadian forces' tactical operations centre of the KPRT, trying to control my nerves. The room was dark, illuminated only by video monitors displaying feeds from high-resolution cameras located near the base. A helium spotting balloon floated over the base like the Goodyear blimp, providing video surveillance. There was constant staticky chatter on the radio from patrols calling in and voices of the soldiers in communication with them.

I was there as a result of a conversation I'd had the previous evening with Terry Hackett, chief of our Correctional Service Canada team.[11] "I need to talk to you about a night patrol tomorrow," he said.

I had not been in the job very long and didn't know what he was talking about. "What's it about? Why are you doing it at night?"

"The Afghan prison service is worried they have too many Taliban detainees in Sarpoza, they need to move them up to the main prison in Kabul. The more prisoners in Sarpoza, the more incentive there is for a prison break," he explained. "They do it at night so people don't see and the streets are quiet." Terry and his staff would be present to ensure humane treatment as the Afghan prison service transported prisoners to KAF where they would be transferred via transport plane to the larger prison in Kabul.

"Sarpoza is the top target in Kandahar city. If the Taliban find out about the transfer, they might try to break them out and get them back in the fight," Terry explained to me. They had done it

---

11. The views expressed by Mr. Hackett in this chapter are his own. They do not constitute the official position of the ICRC or any previous employers.

before. In June 2008, the Taliban had freed 1,200 inmates, killing fifteen guards in the process. And just five months before my arrival, in March 2010, two of his team were caught outside the wire during another attempt, when the Taliban had simultaneously attacked the KPRT, police headquarters, the governor's palace, Sarpoza and an area near Ahmed Wali Karzai's home. It was the biggest attack of the year.

That night Terry was at Sarpoza working with the warden on a PowerPoint presentation for ISAF headquarters when a suicide bomber driving a dump truck smashed into the prison's exterior wall, blowing it up and killing thirty civilians who lived nearby. Terry felt something sharp going into the back of his head as he was blown against the wall—shards of glass projected inward from a shattered window. The warden and Terry's close protection soldier were knocked unconscious. The clang of steel bars rang through the prison as Taliban prisoners shook their cell walls and shouted, sure this was their chance to escape. Terry worried about the other members of his team who were down in the cell block.

Stab A moved fast to block the breach in the wall with a LAV. The Canadian soldiers had night vision gear but held their fire as it was not possible to make positive target identification. The Taliban and Sarpoza guards patrolling the perimeter exchanged fire indiscriminately. "With all the attacks around the city, the Quick Response Force was stuck and didn't get to us for several hours." When help finally arrived, Terry and his team, together with soldiers trained in tactical combat casualty care, provided first aid for injured guards and prisoners. They helped the Afghans with head counts, went back to the KPRT, got stitched up and returned to Sarpoza to help restore order and shore things up, at least temporarily. By that time, it was after midnight—Terry's thirty-fifth birthday.

Now it was my responsibility to approve the night patrol that could put him and Stab A in harm's way. If anything happened, there would be nothing I could do. Still, Terry couldn't do his job if

I second-guessed him. If people thought I didn't have confidence in his judgement, it would undermine his leadership.

My face hardened into a mask that hid my anxiety. "Okay," I said.

"Any time Sarpoza is going through something tough like this, the prison authorities want us there to mentor them." Terry's use of the word "mentor" was deliberate and important. He and his team were providing training and support to help the Afghans to do their job professionally but the prison system was the sole responsibility of the Afghan government. As jails in conflict-ridden failed states like Afghanistan are black holes for human rights, it was a distinction the Canadian government took great pains to emphasize.

Terry had travelled across more than one world to lead the small team of experts from Correctional Service Canada at the KPRT. Before coming to Kandahar, he was warden of a federal minimum-security prison on a remote mountaintop in British Columbia. In fact, it wasn't even called a prison. It was called the Kwìkwèxwelhp Healing Lodge. Community elders guided the healing journey. There were no barriers between residents and staff. He came from a cutting-edge progressive institution dedicated to providing a culturally appropriate environment for the rehabilitation of Indigenous inmates to a third-world prison situated in the middle of a counterinsurgency. "You couldn't get a more extreme contrast. No fences in the forest, you know."

Combining a generous and kind spirit with the tough mindset necessary to excel in a career in corrections, Terry started by learning about Afghan prison culture. There were surprising differences. "In North America, if you accommodate a person in a single cell that is what they want. They want to be by themselves and have privacy. In Afghanistan, if you have single cells you think you're doing something good, but you are violating cultural norms. In Sarpoza we didn't take our preconceived Western concepts and inject them over top."

Terry didn't view or treat prisoners as enemies. Putting human dignity first was the cornerstone of his efforts. "At the end of the day, you are dealing with people. The detainees have families; they have the same basic needs as you and I. We engaged with them based on our shared humanity. They had grievances against the Afghan government from their perspective. My job wasn't to judge. My job was to support the Afghans in treating their inmates according to national and international standards."

As I sat in the tactical operations centre, the call came in that the prisoners had been safely transferred. Terry and his team were on their way back to the KPRT. I admired their dedication and skill, but I never stopped worrying that something could go badly wrong.

A peculiar smell emanates from the stained and mildewed stone walls of Sarpoza prison. A yeasty odour of urine is the olfactory backdrop to an acid scent of fear. The old prison broods on the edge of town like the fortress of a cruel medieval king while, right next to it, the busy commerce of jingle trucks and buses rushes back and forth. The walls of Sarpoza sidle up to the simple dwellings of poor Kandaharis. Prisons are not good neighbours, especially this one.

On a rocky extrusion across the main highway, sub-par for a mountain but a landmark nonetheless, forty stairs are carved into the stone leading to a mysterious cave. On its walls, in Greek and Aramaic, the language of Jesus, an Indian emperor of two millennia ago exhorts his subjects to piety and respect.

I gazed toward the cave from the vaulted stone roof of the prison, then returned my attention to the inmates milling about in the small exercise yard below. I descended to the prison yard to check out the tailoring and woodworking classrooms Canada had equipped to rehabilitate common criminals and Taliban fighters so they could, after serving their time, return as productive members of society.

Walking into the cell blocks felt like walking into a dungeon that had received a makeover. Canada had refurbished the cells, toilets and yards to meet minimum international standards as well as given the place a bright green paint job, a colour that the prisoners chose. That smell stuck around, on top of the others.

Sarpoza was divided into three separate sections. The Taliban detainees were held in the "political block." When I looked through the steel bars, the prisoners fired vengeful scowls my way. On the other side of the prison, criminal offenders paid their dues. They were friendly and relaxed in comparison. A third block held the female prisoners and their children. For those who had money, a small kiosk sold candy and cigarettes.

To make sure the Afghans understood we were serious about the absolute prohibition of torture and the humane treatment of prisoners (for the detainees we transferred, at any rate), I met regularly with the Sarpoza warden, General Mayar. He had replaced the previous warden who was suspected of collaborating with the Taliban and fired on Christmas Day 2009.

General Mayar was trained by the Russians and had managed prisons around the country throughout Afghanistan's political upheavals, retaining the confidence of governments that came and went. He had a large office with a locked, glass-fronted cabinet filled with all kinds and colours of cell phones confiscated from prisoners. Weapons were on display too. The display was meant to show how strict and effective he was but I got the feeling there were others that snuck through.

Mayar's flinty face reflected a hard fifty years with few, if any, occasions to smile. He wore the flat grey-blue uniform of the Afghan prison service and kept a peaked cap on the right-hand side of his imposing wooden desk, close at hand for when he stepped outside of the office. Dominating the desk was a big marble plaque inscribed "Gen. GH Dastgier Mayar, Master of Laws in English and Pashtu." His manner was gruff, stiff and very formal but he got along well with Terry and appreciated the Canadian help. Sarpoza was cleaner, safer and a much better place for prisoners and staff alike than it had ever been before.

Still, no place in Kandahar city was more dangerous and it's hard to imagine a more undesirable job than being a guard in an Afghan prison. The prisoners knew who they were, and so did people in their community. It was as dangerous as being a policeman, except prison guards were unarmed within the walls of the prison. It would be catastrophic if a gun was seized by a prisoner.

The most high-risk situation for prison guards, or police for that matter, is if they feel their lives are in danger. When guards, who are supposed to be the dominant power, panic, they are liable to do anything, including killing prisoners. Containing risky situations while respecting human rights requires proper riot control gear and knowing how to use it.

The training I hated the most, but my Canadian staff loved, was riot simulation. In an enclosed yard within the base, young foreign service officers and members of the Canadian military dressed to get dirty in scruffy old jeans and T-shirts, were given sticks and instructions to go crazy, screaming and rushing the guards as if they were rioting prisoners. Ordinarily mild-mannered diplomats and aid workers behaved like a rugby team of the criminally insane. They enjoyed the direct full contact with Afghans in a game-like situation as well as blowing off steam for a good cause.

The guards had been supplied with plexiglass shields and batons. They had also received several days of theoretical and practical training on how to use the equipment within international legal frameworks on the use of force. Now Terry and his Canadian prison experts, dressed in beige cargo pants and tactical uniform shirts with CSC and KPRT shoulder patches, looked on, coaching the trainees and calling out advice through interpreters.

Every time these fake riots took place, my catastrophic imagination went into overdrive. I kept imagining the trouble I would be in if somebody's nose or arm got broken. But no one was ever hurt during the training—at least, not inside the wire.

After one training session, the recruits were attacked returning to Sarpoza in a van we had provided. "As soon as they left the gate of our camp," Terry said, "there was an explosion just outside the base. The van had been hit by an IED." The destroyed vehicle was perforated by little circular holes made by ball bearings that went through the walls of the van. The base security team whipped out of the gate to retrieve the casualties, and everybody helped apply combat first aid until the wounded could be evacuated to the military hospital at KAF. One recruit was killed and seven had significant injuries.

Despite the efforts of Terry and his team, events in the spring of 2011 made me question the reliability of the institution and partners we were working with.

The Taliban secretly controlled a building site just across the main highway from Sarpoza prison. Because the building was under construction, nobody thought it was strange that dump trucks kept hauling dirt out of the site. In actuality, for five months the Taliban had been digging a 360-metre tunnel to the political block. In the middle of an April night, that tunnel broke through into one of the cells. The other cells were unlocked and almost five hundred prisoners escaped, just in time for the start of fighting season. When they exited the tunnel, prisoners were met by their Taliban commanders and taken away by car. It seems General Mayar hadn't confiscated all the cell phones after all.

It was a grave setback for us and a brilliant success for the Taliban, who proved themselves capable of planning and executing daring and sophisticated operations under the noses of the Afghan government and NATO. The public had not informed on them during construction and now a powerful propaganda effect vibrated across the province. Many Kandaharis blamed corruption and the weakness of the government; Taliban speaking to the press after the escape said the guards in that wing were either asleep or stoned. To me, the unlocked cells, the precise location in which the tunnel penetrated the prison floor and the number of prisoners who escaped before alarms were raised strongly suggested an inside job.

I asked Rambo about the breakout. He told me that "those young guys or older men on one side of the bars and those guards in uniform on the other side, they're from the same village." He added that many people with family members in jail were happy with the breakout and pointed out that not everyone was guilty. "There were people in Sarpoza because they had Afghan army commanders after them who wanted them in jail for reasons unrelated to the war."

In the KPRT, we were devastated by the news. The American reinforcements were taking over and the Canadian forces were in the last year of a much more manageable job. The end of our mission was coming into sight and it had gone pretty well for us this last year. We were completing our targets, my team was getting its job done, none of them had been seriously injured and Dean told me military casualties were down. Now some in the KPRT worried that Taliban tunnels might start popping up in our bedrooms or bathrooms.

The angry American general commanding RC South asked me, "Weren't the Canadians in charge of the prison?"

We were indeed taking the lead in improving the prison but the US had taken over responsibility for security in Kandahar city. "We weren't responsible for the security of the prison," said Terry, who only had two months left to go when the breakout occurred. "The Afghans were. By that point, the Americans had a permanent footprint at Sarpoza as part of the handover. They had built a rule-of-law base at the site."

General Mayar, along with some of his guards, was arrested and placed in preventive custody at the National Directorate of Security, the internal intelligence agency. A little bit later, during one of our regular visits there to check Canadian detainees, he tried to wave the monitor over—in vain. We did not monitor detainees who were not captured by Canada.

# CHAPTER TWELVE

# COURTS, COPS AND CORRECTIONS

Of the thousands of Afghan police Canada trained, I remember the women most vividly. Faces sunburnt from being on the beat, they trained at the facility we built within Camp Nathan Smith. Shooting practice was conducted at the firing range near my office. Dressed in black combat boots, a blue hijab and dark ballistic glasses, they would adopt a straight-arm shooting stance as demonstrated by their Canadian policewomen trainers. Firmly gripping their nine-millimetre automatic pistols in two hands adorned in elaborate henna designs, they levelled steely glares at targets of charging enemy fighters and aimed for the chest. After emptying their magazine, they went up to the targets and counted their kill shots with pride.

Women made up only one percent of the police in Afghanistan, a modest but necessary start in such a male-dominated environment. At the end of the training course, I would join them in the conference room of the KPRT police training centre. Standing by the lectern with the black-bearded male Afghan commander on my right, and his slim and fit female counterpart on my left, I handed out framed certificates of completion. After accepting their awards with shy smiles, they turned to their comrades and proudly raised them high above their heads to hearty applause.

The Canadian civilian police were part of an ambitious NATO plan to recruit, train and assign 134,000 policemen and women throughout Afghanistan by October 2011. The RCMP was given a leadership role, along with the Italian Carabinieri, French

Gendarmerie, Czech National Police and trainers from ten other countries. Canadian police are in high demand for international assignments like this because of their professionalism, advanced training and democratic values. They are among the best in the world.

The RCMP has an international police training program that recruits seasoned officers like Joe McAllister from provincial and big-city services across the country. In 2007, Joe was running a thirty-officer shift in Surrey, BC when he got the call to go to Afghanistan. Policing in war zones was not new to him: he had already been on UN missions in Kosova and East Timor. But even his experience did not prepare him for the friction, complexity and danger of re-establishing the Afghan National Police. "The most challenging part was trying to figure out the different roles. You had some people who just wanted to train the ANP to fight the war and then you had some people who wanted to build their capacity," Joe said.

The commander of our ten-person police contingent, Joe has the strength of physical presence and direct personality we associate with police. He and his team wore uniforms the same sand colour as the troops, but without the pixelated camouflage. Each had a shoulder patch that read "Canadian Police, Task Force Kandahar." Over that was a patch with the insignia of their particular service. Joe was RCMP; services such as the Toronto Police were also represented. They were armed with a pistol strapped to their leg, and outside the wire they carried the same C7 assault rifle as the troops.

International policing was not new to Afghanistan. King Mohammad Zahir Shah brought in the Germans to help him set up the Afghan police force in the 1960s and 70s. Germany established a training academy in Kabul in 1989. Once trained, officers were integrated with the traditional decentralized power structure of tribes and tribal leaders: the police gave their allegiance to the local chief to avoid becoming a source of conflict between the king's government and the tribes. The system worked well for forty years, then fell apart because of the Afghan–Soviet war.

Joe's first challenge on the job was delineating the roles of the army and the police. Theoretically, once the Afghan and Canadian military had cleared a district of Taliban fighters, they would hold the ground while the civilian police force established order. In reality, military operations and police work intermingled, especially as the US emphasized a combat role for the police. "The Americans we dealt with just wanted them to go out there and shoot Taliban," Joe explained. The government of Afghanistan agreed, putting the police in the fight.

When Joe first arrived in 2007, "these poorly trained and equipped men were out there fighting the enemy and taking casualties, and we're trying to teach them about their role in the community. I think that slowed progress down a lot because the Kandahar police chief was caught between those two things."

Joe tried to move policing closer to the community. "They didn't know they had another role," he explained. "So I took these guys out on foot patrols in Kandahar city. I told them 'You have three questions to ask here: Do you feel safe? How can I help you? Do you know how to call me if you need help?' Just ask those three questions."

With that kind of engagement, the relationship with the community began to shift. Joe showed the police how to connect with kids. "It's always fun when you're dealing with children. You're giving them a future." The Canadians showed the Afghan police their role in schools, and how to perform it. "I really loved visiting the schools and trying to get the police officers to understand their roles there, to educate the children on land mine awareness and traffic safety and how to avoid drugs, you know, all that type of stuff."

Joe thought the basic Afghan legal and organizational structures for the police were good, but recognized there was a big problem when it came to recruiting police in their thousands. "Uniformed officers on the street could not read or write. They had a gun but were unable to check identification or write a report. So they were mostly used as guards at checkpoints, protecting infrastructure."

Even the best laws could not overcome the cultural limitations. "Afghans don't believe in central government. They believe in their tribe and their tribal leader. So whoever's in charge of their tribe, their community, if that person said stand up and fight, they stood up and fought. If he said sit down, they sat down."

In one district, everybody knew that the local police chief was a corrupt warlord who had used his tribal leadership and influence to get his job. The Kandahar chief of police wanted to fire him. "But he couldn't. If he did, all the police in that district would quit. Their loyalty was to that guy."

Corruption was endemic in the Afghan National Police. The first provincial chief of police Joe worked with was Sayed Aqa Saqib, a burly and grizzled general with a reputation for corruption. He was fired in connection with the 2008 Taliban mass prison break. On top of that, Joe said, "He actually got caught red-handed when they finally found where he put everything he stole."

Saqib was replaced by Matiullah Qati, a respected Kandahari who, unlike his predecessor, took the job out of national duty, pride in his Pashtun culture and a desire to keep his people safe. Matiullah was the Afghan partner Joe worked the most closely with. "After I got to know him, we got to be buddies and understood each other's role. Then we got to the hand-holding stage." Joe and Matiullah would walk around police headquarters holding hands, a signal from Matiullah to his men that Joe was a trusted and valuable partner. Joe was initially uncomfortable but came to appreciate the gesture of friendship and trust.

Joe also came to understand that the Afghan police chiefs were in a practically impossible position. Matiullah was a caring person who often spoke with sadness about the bad actors engaged in criminal activities in Kandahar. He wanted to do the right thing, but his hands were usually tied for cultural or political reasons. This frustrating reality was not something either of them could change, even though it badly needed changing.

For police from rigorously ethical services, it took a mind shift to accept that some corruption was inevitable. If hungry underpaid police made farmers give them a watermelon to pass through a checkpoint, that was tolerable. But more serious infractions were corrosive. It was a question of where to draw the line.

In June 2009, Matiullah drew the line with a man named Assadullah. Details of his identity, official role and the nature of his crime remain unclear. What is undisputed, however, is that, as soon as he was arrested by the provincial prosecutor, forty-one armed men arrived and demanded the release of their comrade. When Matiullah refused, the argument got heated, a gunfight broke out and Matiullah was killed, along with one of his detectives and four of his men.

The Afghan government blamed the US, saying the gunmen were security guards hired by the US military. The US maintained they were policemen under the jurisdiction of the Afghan Ministry of the Interior. The commander of the Canadian forces at the time, Brigadier General Jonathan Vance, said, "They were members of Afghan security forces." His officials later clarified that the suspects were members of a special unit that supported US counterterror operations.

Joe thinks the men who killed Matiullah were attached to an ISAF special forces unit. "Shot by your own guys, that's pretty hard to take," he said. As far as he knows, the case of Matiullah's killing was never resolved, even though all forty-one men were arrested at the scene. "Those guys don't talk to anybody," Joe said.

After Joe was reassigned to ISAF in Kabul in 2010, Superintendent Vic Park commanded the last and largest civilian police contingent at the KPRT. Vic speaks with a gentle Newfoundland lilt. An attentive listener, he enters conversations respectfully, patiently reserving opinions until he hears the full story. After serving in remote Saskatchewan Indigenous communities, "I moved to the pointy end of the stick for four years," becoming an operator with the RCMP Special Emergency Response Unit, which entailed sniper and assaulter roles.

Vic was on the National Security Team in Toronto during the investigation, arrest and subsequent prosecution of the Toronto 18, a terror plot intended to get Canada out of Afghanistan. The men convicted tried to import three tons of ammonium nitrate and planned to blow up the Toronto Stock Exchange and the Canadian Security and Intelligence Service. They also planned to behead Prime Minister Stephen Harper. "Luckily, we nipped that one in the bud," Vic said. His next job was leading Canada's National Emergency Response Team.

Commanding the Canadian civilian police in Kandahar was perfect for Vic. "I had twenty-nine years of police experience. I had a strong tactical background. I was an adrenaline junkie. Afghanistan kind of grabbed me," he said. His wife was supportive but worried. His two adult daughters were afraid for him. When he phoned, his daughters would say, "Dad, you should come home."

Vic's job was all-consuming. He had thirty-two civilian police from Canadian police services deployed across Kandahar province: there were seventeen trainers at the police training centre at Forward Operating Base Walton, one each in Dand and Panjwai and thirteen rotating through seventeen police substations in Kandahar city. Vic's most significant contribution to the Canadian civilian police mission was supplementing the training of patrol officers conducted at the KPRT with a training program for senior officers, the first time such an opportunity was offered outside of the police academy in Kabul.

One of Vic's primary challenges was doing the job blindfolded. "When you're executing a warrant in Canada, you just get in your car, watch it unfold and support your people if they need it. In Kandahar, communication was pretty much nil. My people were on their own. That was a big stressor for me." In Canada, police are mobile. In Kandahar, "we were at the beck and call of the Canadian forces or American army to go anywhere." Overcoming obstacles was the name of the game. Training approaches that worked in Canada made no sense for Afghan police. Vic got around the literacy problem by teaching the police to take pictures at a crime scene and dictating observations into a recorder. "We always found a way to make things happen the best we could."

With his people dispersed across the province, Vic worried about burnout and PTSD and made a point of visiting the staff in the field. "There was a lot of stuff going down in Dand and Panjwai. Long firefights pinned Canadian police mentors down behind walls a couple of different times." Those intense periods made the isolation harder, and his visits were welcome. "Basically, it was a health check. I asked them 'What's going on? How are things going, are we on mission or not?'" On a visit to Dand, one of his officers said to him, "It's so nice that someone came down to see me. I haven't seen anyone in three months."

A Canadian policewoman from Thompson, Manitoba, was leading a routine foot patrol, teaching community policing in Panjwai, when a Canadian Chinook helicopter was shot down right in front of them. This wasn't mentoring; now they were on a rescue mission. As they ran to the helicopter, she and her patrol took fire. Combat wasn't her job, but she couldn't leave her squad. Afterward, Vic had to be decisive. "You've taken on a military role and this can't happen. Pack your bags, you're coming back with me," he said. The base commander was switched out because the line between police mentoring and combat operations had become blurred.

Similarly, as soon as he saw officers not coping, he sent them home. "If they weren't a good fit for the sandbox, these people were going to be a hazard to themselves and a hazard to everyone around them."

The hardest part of the job was working outside the wire all the time. "No place was safe. Inside a compound you had rocket attacks and mortar attacks. A car bomb went off at Camp Nathan Smith when I was doing a presentation," Vic said. With his experience in counterterrorism and emergency response, Vic thought he was crisis-proof. But Kandahar drained the stamina out of him and other experienced crisis managers. "The place never shut off. Day or night. You were in a full-blown war zone every minute and everywhere that you went."

On Saturday, February 12, 2011, the risk became immediate as the result of another signature Taliban attack. Right after lunch, Taliban fighters positioned on the second floor of an adjacent hotel rained fire down on the Kandahar city police headquarters with AK47s, rocket-propelled grenades and hand grenades as four suicide bombers drove to the gates. Three detonated. One was shot and captured before he could blow himself up. I could see the plume of grey smoke from my office.

The battle lasted four hours. Two Canadian police officers were with American soldiers at the time and returned suppressing fire, as well as helping with the treatment and transportation of the casualties. NATO reported that nineteen Afghans, including two civilians, were killed. Forty-nine people were wounded, including twenty-three civilians, of whom nine were children. Canadian civilian police shared the risks of their Afghan counterparts and their Canadian forces colleagues. There was simply no way to do the job otherwise.

Police officers weren't the only Taliban targets. Anyone who worked for the government of Afghanistan was vulnerable, even if theirs was an ordinary non-political job. The head of the prison registry, who just recorded the names and release dates of inmates, was killed. Blunting the sharpness of the relentless Taliban assassination campaign was another of the responsibilities that fell to Phil Lupul.

As a successor to Richard Colvin, Phil also sought to honour the

CHAPTER TWELVE: COURTS, COPS AND CORRECTIONS

sacrifice of Glyn Berry by contributing capacity that the military was not designed to have. Like me, Phil was in his fifties when he came to Kandahar. Trained as a lawyer, he had been working as a manager in Canada's immigration and consular program with a focus on justice and security. "We used to call it the three Cs: Courts, Cops and Corrections." When Canada started advertising for volunteers to go to Kandahar, Phil decided this would be the kind of offbeat and adventurous assignment that he liked.

Phil's political section of ten staff was larger than its counterparts in all but the biggest Canadian embassies. In addition to understanding the political scene in which we operated, it was responsible for administering the detainee monitoring program and providing the infrastructure the government of Kandahar needed to function.

Phil's team built protected office spaces in Kandahar city, in the district centres and in the governor's palace. They installed fencing and security measures around courthouses so that the justice sector could operate safe from Taliban attack. To protect government workers, they refurbished an abandoned housing compound where Mullah Omar, the previous leader of the Taliban, had lived. The compound was hardened with perimeter security and turned into safe housing for government officials and their families.

Turning the former home of Mullah Omar into a residence for Afghan government officials wasn't just practical. In an environment long defined by competing militias, it sent a message that the government was in control and not afraid to show its presence.

# CHAPTER THIRTEEN

## TELLING THE STORY

"Sir, we just got the decision about you speaking to the press at the opening of the Police Training Centre," Katherine Heath-Eves said. "You can't do it."

I was angry. "Come on, Katherine, are you sure? Can we push back?"

We were transferring the police training centre we built at Camp Nathan Smith, and the responsibility for its administration, to the Afghan government. It was an unmitigated good news story about Canada empowering Afghans to take responsibility for Afghan security.

The ceremony would be that afternoon. In front of the training facility, a stage with a lectern had been set up for me, the governor, the chief of police and other speakers. Afghan, Canadian and US flags formed the backdrop. Rows of folding chairs were set up on the gravel for an audience that included Canadian forces, US officers and Canadian, international and Afghan press. I had written and rehearsed a very good speech.

"This is from the Prime Minister's Office," Katherine said. It's a different kind of dangerous to push back on the PMO—doing so can have lifelong career consequences. More than that, if you lose the confidence of the PMO, you can't do your job.

Ben Rowswell had enjoyed full freedom to speak to the press and was good at it. He told me, "RoCKs had a role to explain to Canadians why we were there and why it was worth it, amid all the violence. The Harper government had serious message control over its mission in Afghanistan. There were only seven people in the entire government of Canada who could speak freely to the press about it. The Prime Minister was one of them and I was one of them."

My experience was different. A federal election was coming up in May 2011, and during an election period message discipline is rigid as the government tries to shape the media cycle in its political interest. Canadians supported the government on Afghanistan but that support was trending down and communications were too politically sensitive to let us use our judgement in the field. Messages were under the tight control of the Privy Council Office, even though we were on the other side of the world.

Afghanistan was not the message that the government wanted in the media cycle on that day. The Prime Minister would be making his last visit in May to thank the troops and tell the Canadian people what we had achieved. So I should shut up. When Canadian, Afghan and US press asked me for remarks, I gave them a copy of my pre-cleared speech. But I couldn't say anything on the record.

It was humiliating.

Katherine was one of two young communications professionals on our team. The other was Adam Sweet, a compact, fit and energetic young man whose short-cropped black beard made him look a little bit older than he was. They were both Albertans, but their personalities couldn't have been more different. Adam was exuberant and interested in everything but took setbacks hard. Katherine was impeccably poised, having mastered a prudent professionalism finely attuned to the operation of large government systems.

As a kid, Katherine liked climbing trees and reading books, especially *The Chronicles of Narnia*, in which an intrepid girl named Lucy goes through a mysterious wardrobe to a strange world and ends up liberating the magical land of Narnia from an evil witch holding it in perpetual winter. She studied English literature and then got a graduate degree in journalism from Carleton University in Ottawa.

Recruited directly into the parliamentary bureau of *The Globe and Mail*, she was energized by meeting and working with people who shared her interests in politics and world affairs. But the day-to-day grind of journalism was not for her, so she moved into communications with the federal government and went after jobs with travel. Her ability to relate to journalists landed her a job at Foreign Affairs and then a posting to Kandahar.

"I didn't know a lot about Afghanistan. I had a book on my bookshelf called *The World's Most Dangerous Places*. Afghanistan was the most dangerous, and I said to myself, 'Yeah. Let's go there.' Naively, I was not nervous. I just wanted to be there. I was motivated."

Adam grew up in a small town in Alberta. Although he still goes back to visit his mom, he wanted more. While in university, two of his political science professors inspired him to get into international work. "Get an internship," one of them told him.

"Where should I go?" Adam said.

"Washington."

Adam didn't believe him. "Sure. I'll go to Washington where the Washington jobs hang on the Washington tree and just go collect them." He went to Washington and was hired as an intern at the Canadian Embassy.

After Washington, Adam's enterprising nature took him to Ottawa where he started knocking on doors. Initially hired by MP Mike Lake, he was quickly brought on by the Minister of Human Resources and Social Development, fellow Albertan Monte Solberg. He learned how government worked from the partisan political angle until Solberg decided not to run in the 2008 campaign.

Adam was out of a job just as Afghanistan was sweeping over the public service like a tidal wave and departments were scrambling to get qualified staff. His former supervisor in Washington, now working on the communications effort with the CIDA, offered him a job explaining the mission to Canadians.

Adam didn't really know anything about Afghanistan, but that was okay. He supported and attended focus groups that the Department of National Defence was conducting to find out how Canadians felt about the military mission and how to improve their perception of it.

"When you told Canadians what we were doing militarily, they didn't really respond to it. Counterinsurgency combat didn't align with their paradigm of what the Canadian military should be doing." Canadians did not want to take part in the US-led war in Iraq or any heavy-handed military approach to solving international problems.

Canada's development response was shaped to be focused on three very big projects with social goals that Canadians would understand and get behind. "The signature projects were really helpful—three easy-to-remember things: irrigation, schools and polio vaccination," said Adam. People would say 'Okay, that sounds nice.'"

To broaden engagement beyond traditional press releases, Adam and the communication professionals came up with "home-towners," matching small-town papers with stories about local residents. Viola Cassis was one example. "Hey, did you know Viola from Lethbridge is in Kandahar right now working on the maternal-child health program?" Adam asked the editor of the local paper.

"We had no idea."

So Adam set up an interview and sent the *Lethbridge Herald* a picture of Viola surrounded by burka-clad Afghan mothers with their babies at a Canadian maternal and child healthcare project. The next morning it was on the front page and everybody in Lethbridge saw what Canada was doing in Kandahar. Canada was helping mothers and babies.

At first, the government message managers were not very happy about losing control, but local stories were a manageable risk. Adam went on to be the lead for Question Period for CIDA's Afghanistan task force. His job was to think of every conceivable question the opposition might ask to trip the government up and come up with answers that were accurate, informative and defensible.

Adam was thriving in this political pressure cooker, happy to be working on meaningful issues. But when some temporary assignments opened up in Kabul and Kandahar, he headed to the field, where the action was. "Canada was standing tall on the world stage. And I wanted to be part of that, you know? You bet I was going to go over." He and his friend, Joffre LeBlanc, our District Stabilization Officer, were the two youngest civilians sent to Kandahar. Adam was the only one of my civilian staff who always called me "sir."

I usually saw Adam together with Katherine and they were a great pair. Both provided strategic communication advice to the civilian team, including me, and I trusted them both implicitly. Adam focused on showing Canadians that we were helping Afghans. "When Canadians saw that the military mission was working with Foreign Affairs, CIDA, the correctional service and Canadian police we saw tremendous jumps in support," Adam said. But getting that message out proved exceedingly difficult.

Katherine worked with international journalists to showcase Canada's role and capabilities when it came to civilian work. "I wanted to get outside the wire as much as I could, and I always loved going to Sarpoza. It was a big project, representative of our efforts to stabilize the country and give the people of Kandahar a sense of security and confidence in their government. I would show international journalists the infrastructure improvements and explain how we were building up the capabilities of the prison guards and even the warden himself."

Katherine was touring Sarpoza prison with a CNN correspondent when one of the corrections experts warned her of the imminent threat of a truck bomb. "We've shut down the gates," he explained. Despite his assurances, Katherine and the correspondent were standing in the prison yard when the gates opened and she heard the beep-beep-beep of a truck backing up. "I thought, 'This is it. The truck is going to explode.' I was sure that was the end of us." Instead, the back tilted and a load of gravel slid out.

The danger always felt real, even when it was a false alarm. Still, Katherine said, "The toughest part of my job was dealing with Ottawa. Say we have a reporter who was ready to go outside the wire. You've educated them about the project they're going to see. They are planning to do a story. They have buy-in from their editor back home. There's a helicopter, there's a convoy. You have done a ton of work and mapped it all out. Then, when everything is all ready, it's time to ask Ottawa for approval." All too often, "they would turn it down based on some stupid reason. A political whim."

The Canadian forces understood and supported Katherine's work. When she started her posting in 2010, she sat down with General Vance and explained she wanted journalists to see what Canadians were doing to bring irrigation to Kandahar farmers. "You're right. Let's get some journalists out there," he said. He followed through by providing the armoured convoy to make it happen; four Canadian correspondents got out in the field to see one of Canada's signature projects.

Getting Canadian journalists to KAF was one thing. Getting them out in the field to see Canada's work firsthand turned out to be something altogether different for many reasons. "Number one was insurance for journalists," Adam explained. "If you can even get life or health insurance in a war zone, it is extremely expensive and incredibly limiting, so editors did not want to send journalists outside the wire. This was a Canadian problem. This was not an American problem. This was not an international media problem. It was a Canadian media problem. They had to get permission from their editors to go outside the wire and they rarely got that permission. So they would stay in KAF."

If journalists did go outside the wire, they preferred to be with soldiers on patrol rather than touring the development and governance projects Adam wanted to profile. And security concerns made destinations like schools and clinics off-limits—rolling up in military vehicles would have made them targets for the Taliban.

Ramp ceremonies were another reason. When a Canadian soldier died, it made the news four times. There was an announcement from the Canadian forces when it happened. Then the body was repatriated with a ramp ceremony, always at night: the casket, draped in a Canadian flag, was carried by his or her closest comrades past Canadian and multinational soldiers standing in formation on the runway apron, then up the ramp of the military transport plane for return to Canada. After the plane landed at Canadian Forces Base Trenton, the remains of the fallen were driven with honours down the 170-kilometre stretch of Hwy 401 known as the "Highway of Heroes" to the office of the Ontario Chief Coroner in Toronto. Finally, there was the family funeral itself.

We would have a shadow ramp ceremony in the small Camp Nathan Smith parade ground at the same time as the one in KAF, thirty-three kilometres away. I never had to tell our team to attend; everybody wanted to be there. It was a matter of respect and honour to film and share with Canadians the ultimate sacrifices that were made. But it also shaped the story into one of tragedy and sacrifice. Canadian journalists, especially television journalists, needed to catch the ramp ceremonies for the nightly news, and that kept them on the base.

The late Matthew Fisher of Postmedia was a notable exception. He was often at the KPRT and consistently out covering events. When he went on leave in December 2009, the *Calgary Herald* sent Michelle Lang out to cover for him.

Adam will never forget Michelle. "She was unsure about leaving KAF and was pretty nervous. But we were convinced of the importance of showing Canadians the development mission to highlight the larger picture of why we were there and to increase support for the effort. So I went to KAF and spent a lot of time sitting down and saying, 'We're going to go to Dand district and you are going to see the model villages. You can come to the KPRT and talk about the Dahla Dam project.' All those sorts of things. We convinced her to come over to the KPRT."

Adam and Michelle were both on the manifest for LAV Alpha. "There were two convoys, Alpha and Charlie. I knew one of the reservists on Alpha was a teacher from Alberta, like Michelle. I thought a good story might come from that." At the last minute, Michelle was reassigned to LAV Charlie and Adam was bumped by Sergeant Kirk Taylor, who was accompanying Bushra.

In addition to Canadian and international audiences, it was critical to demonstrate to Afghan citizens that things were getting better, that the country was safer and developing, that the government of Afghanistan was back in charge. Adam coached the governor's spokesman, Dr. Najib, on how to get that message out in alignment with communications from Canada and NATO using the new Government Media and Information Centre, the crown jewel in Phil Lupul's suite of projects.

The media centre had transformative potential in Kandahar. "Essentially it was a TV and radio studio so that the government could get its message out to its citizens. It also had the capacity to link up national and local level government together for video conferencing," Phil explained.

A medical doctor, Dr. Najib was young, maybe four years older than Adam. "Dr. Najib was simultaneously one of the most brave, courageous, intelligent, annoying and frustrating people I've ever worked with," Adam said. Food was one of his great loves and he worried about his weight, though his baggy salwar kameez hid it well. He struggled with English and often wore a grumpy face. Then, "God, he would have this great smile. We would get excited about something, or we would talk and this light would come on inside him. It recharged me. I thought, 'We have something here.

We can move something forward.' He was passionate about telling people the good work that was going on, otherwise it would be invisible to them."

However, the international mission also frustrated Dr. Najib. "He was incredibly patient with our continual screw-ups," including being shot in the foot by an American soldier when he refused to submit to a humiliating pat down before entering his own office at the governor's palace.

A more typical example was the Hamkari campaign intended to emphasize the growing effectiveness of the government of Kandahar, particularly concerning reconstruction. The KPRT team, led by Adam's predecessor, Farhaan, worked with Dr. Najib on the rollout, creating a robust public relations campaign. "We were creating a new kind of marketing campaign. It was positive and talked about development. We even handed out Hamkari-themed swinging ornaments for rear-view mirrors. And jingle things for jingle trucks, all kinds of different stuff."

The original planning meeting brought all the commanders and senior civilians together in the packed KPRT conference room. All the money and all the countries made things more complicated, more cumbersome and more expensive. Farhaan was there and calculated the salaries of the attendees, the cost of the Black Hawks and transportation to move everyone to the KPRT, plus the hourly salary of everybody assembled, to establish the roll-out plan. The meeting cost over a million dollars for three hours. Worse, nobody came up with a plan.

Just asking the Afghans what they wanted and needed to get the messages out would have been better. Farhaan shared with the team that he had been texting with Dr. Najib, who was at the Governor's palace, that the Afghans had met for five minutes and had come up with a plan that was already going ahead. "The Afghans were just like—away we go. Here's the problem. Fix it, move on. There's no time to waste."

Despite their best efforts, a deep contradiction between civilian reconstruction and military expediency smouldered under all that Adam and Dr. Najib were trying to accomplish. Visible changes to the urban landscape demonstrated that Canada was working with the government of Kandahar to deliver a better future but "every night, all people heard were Black Hawks raiding people's houses."

Special forces soldiers used night raids to round up high-value Taliban commanders and bomb makers by creeping up on a family compound using night-vision goggles or by swooping down in a helicopter. The targets would be taken prisoner—in front of their wives, mothers and children—or killed if they didn't surrender. It was effective and arguably safer for civilians, but it was too much for the Afghan sensibility: the sanctity of the home was violated, women were exposed to the eyes of infidel foreigners and children were traumatized. After years of protest, President Karzai announced a ban on night raids and house searches in November 2011 with little effect. ISAF considered the raids essential to operations.

The case of Tarok Kolache was another haunting example of how a legitimate military operation was horribly wrong from a communications point of view. In October 2010, there was heavy fighting between the US Army and the Taliban in the district of Arghandab. Before the Taliban retreated from their stronghold in the hamlet of Tarok Kolache, they booby-trapped the reportedly empty houses of the villagers.

The US commander in charge, Lieutenant Colonel David Flynn, planned an air strike. Adam and Dr. Najib both said, "Don't do this, even though there's nobody there. We know this, you know this, but everybody else is going to see you bombing a village and the Taliban are going to take advantage of it. And they were like, 'Nope. Dropping the bombs.'"

Twenty-five tons of bombs were dropped on an area not much bigger than a soccer field with predictable results: the village was literally turned to dust. Plans were made to rebuild it, but that didn't change public perception. The US had laid waste to an Afghan village.

Empty Afghan houses were routinely demolished to reduce the risks to US soldiers from hidden bombs. Counterinsurgency officer Howard Coombs cites another example, also in the Arghandab district. The Americans had taken a lot of casualties so they brought in a fearsome tool called the MICLIC (Mine Clearing Line Charge) that used a rocket to fire a tube full of explosives to detonate mines and create a ten-metre-wide safe lane for troop movements.

US troops bombed their way forward. "They would warn the villagers, and everybody else in the way. And then they would fire the MICLICs." It was a tactic guaranteed to alarm and upset every farmer and family in the zone they wanted to stabilize. "They increased the danger to their own soldiers," Howard maintains, "because every Kandahari who could pick up a rifle headed in that direction. In the Canadian area of operations, we actually had a noticeable drop in incidents during this period because they all headed for the Americans. US casualties spiked because they were getting attacked all the time." From a messaging point of view, it wasn't a tactic that conveyed the intent to reconstruct.

Sometimes communications were derailed by international events. On March 20, 2011, an anti-Muslim stunt in Florida created havoc in Kandahar city and around the country. Terry Jones, pastor of the small and obscure Dove World Outreach Center in Gainesville, soaked a copy of the Quran in kerosene and set it on fire.

Jones had been threatening to do this for months "to punish Islam" and kept cranking up the dramatic suspense of his ugly political theatre. The Center has signs in front of its little chapel that read "Islam is the Devil." The tension rose day by day and the threat of desecration was all over the international and Afghan press. President Barak Obama, Secretary of Defense Robert Gates and General David Petraeus, Commander of NATO forces in

Afghanistan, all warned that lives would be put in danger by this reckless act of Islamophobia. I simply couldn't believe that the US government could not make Pastor Jones back down.

It's a strange feeling when an act of ignorant craziness on the other side of the world has the potential to ignite fatal violence all around you. The KPRT was an innocent bystander, but we dreaded the message this sent to the pious Afghans. The internet spread the incendiary message around the world at the speed of light. International staff from all UN agencies left their compounds and came to stay with us in relative safety. We cancelled patrols outside the wire, hoping for the best as outraged Afghans took to the streets.

Violent protests in Kandahar province left twelve people dead and 110 wounded. Muslim religious leaders made their hostility to the international mission clear, describing all Afghans who worked with foreigners as traitors and calling for all foreign military bases to be closed. President Karzai issued a statement "strongly denounc[ing] the desecration of Holy Quran by US Preacher in Florida, [and calling] on the US and the United Nations to bring to justice the perpetrators of this crime and provide a satisfactory response to the resentment and anger of over 1.5 billion Muslims around the world."

We didn't know how bad it could get until, on April Fool's Day, the UN compound in Mazar-e-Sharif in the north of the country was overrun by demonstrators armed with knives and guns. They killed seven international staff: four Gurkha security guards and three international UN staff members.

Pastor Terry Jones said he was not to blame. To follow up, he promised to put the life of the Prophet Mohammad on trial.

The following month, we were again on high alert because of an event in another country. After a decade of searching for Osama Bin Laden, the author of the terror attack on the US that started this war, the US found and killed him next door in

Pakistan. I didn't feel it at the time, but now I see that killing Bin Laden diminished the strategic urgency of state-bulding and development in Afghanistan.

Rambo said most people in Kandahar were happy: Bin Laden was an Arab who had brought nothing but trouble to Afghanistan. It was good he was killed. I was pretty convinced that Kandaharis were not going to mourn Bin Laden but the front lines of the heart are hard to map. I hoped that our work was encouraging Kandaharis to feel better and better about the future, but it was an uncertain guess. A survey by the International Council on Security and Development released shortly after Bin Laden's death gave fresh and reliable information on what Afghan men thought about the conflict and the NATO campaign.[12]

There was some good news. Most Kandaharis were indeed happy that Bin Laden was killed. Educated people in cities believed that NATO and the Afghan government were winning. But on the front lines, in districts like Panjwai, most respondents thought the Taliban was winning. A slight majority (53%) of people in southern Afghanistan were ready for the Taliban to be reintegrated into their communities and for the war to end.

But most Afghan men interviewed (79% in southern Afghanistan) said they felt sad or angry regularly. A majority (69%) blamed foreign forces for the bulk of civilian deaths. Most discouraging of all, 91% of respondents in the south did not believe that NATO forces respected Afghan religion and traditions.

Canada delivered aid and support to Kandahar that was significant and appreciated. But stories of reconstruction and development were often overshadowed by other events that dominated the daily life of Kandaharis. Conflicting civilian and military priorities, multinational stakeholders, logistical issues that threatened personal safety, and external geopolitical forces all conspired to make a hard job harder.

12. "Afghanistan Transition: The Death of Bin Laden and Local Dynamics," The International Council on Security and Development (ICOS), May 2011

On the home front, Ottawa wanted to shape the way our efforts were perceived to suit a domestic agenda. I was frustrated because it seemed partisan politics were blocking out information Canadians deserved. I got it, but I didn't agree with it.

## Chapter Fourteen

## Toward a Tipping Point

In January 2011, I flew to Panjwai for a ceremony that was simultaneously humiliating and respectful. Accompanied by Dean Milner, his American counterpart and our civilian leadership, I was seated next to the current district governor, Haji Shah Baran Khaksar, as he introduced his successor, Haji Fazluddin Agha, to one hundred fifty elders sitting on the carpeted floor of the district centre.

Haji is an honorific bestowed on those who have completed the pilgrimage to Mecca in Saudi Arabia, a mark of both piety and status. A member of the Noorzai tribe, Haji Baran was a larger-than-life figure renowned for his bombast. Haji Fazluddin Agha was a tribal leader with a large tract of land and a substantial family compound. More importantly, he had experience leading other districts, including strategic Spin Boldak, on the border with Pakistan. Like Haji Baran, Haji Fazluddin had a full black beard. His dark eyes squinted with wary cunning and flashed with energetic determination. He carried himself with a sense of gravitas, his imposing belly lending physical presence to his short stature.

I listened to the simultaneous translation through earphones as Haji Baran explained that he was stepping down but would remain in the district to lend his support to the new district governor. We took the opportunity to thank and recognize Haji Baran, though his accomplishments had fallen short of our ambitions.

Haji Baran looked baffled as he listened to Fazluddin Agha thunder like the baritone in a heroic opera, exhorting the elders to come onside in the fight against the Taliban and join in the development of their district. "I will try my best to convince those (Taliban) brothers who are upset to come and join us in the peace process," Agha said. "I will give them every guarantee that they will not be harmed. They can live here. They can do their work. Any still causing violence and problems, I am against them and I will try my best, with all possible means, to root them out and arrest them."

The role of the district governor was to develop a livable consensus through community consultation at gatherings called *shuras,* and to bring government services, like education and health, into Panjwai. Our District Stabilization Officer, Joffre LeBlanc, operated as the district governor's chief of staff, liaising with the military and aid programs, communicating with the provincial government, and organizing shuras and media interviews.

I first met Joffre in September. He had flown into the KPRT from Panjwai for a meeting with the governor and his ministers to plan reconstruction projects in his district and stopped by my office to give me a preliminary briefing. His manner was cautious. His fine features were animated and sharp, with piercing brown eyes. His sandy brown hair was receding a little, even though he was just twenty-six.

"Hi, Joffre. How's it going in Panjwai?"

Joffre paused to calibrate his words. "I'm trying to work with the district governor to implement governance, giving him some support in taking on those responsibilities."

"What's he like, Haji Baran? Is it true about the teapot?"

"I'm just getting to know him. I would describe him as mercurial. He's illiterate. He gets frustrated sometimes. He yells and swears at the elders. He hit somebody with a shovel. And yes, he had a disagreement with his chief of police and hit him with a steel teapot. It drew some blood."

It was hard not to laugh a little about that.

"How is he with you?"

"He's been kind to me," Joffre said. "But this isn't going to be easy."

Joffre was a former reserve intelligence officer who later joined Foreign Affairs as an advisor with the Afghanistan Task Force. He hoped to join the Kandahar mission as a political officer, where he could use his analytical skills to decipher meaning out of the fog of war and shape the planning of military operations.

The call to work in Kandahar had come just before Christmas 2009. "I'm wondering if you would be willing to work outside the wire, in Panjwai," the personnel officer said. "With your background, we think you would be a good fit." Joffre was being offered a job in the homeland of the Taliban. "Take some time to think about it over the holidays," she said.

When, just before New Year's Eve, news of the deadly IED attack broke, "maybe half of those civilians selected to go to Kandahar declined," Joffre said, "even though the risk level hadn't changed. I felt compelled to play a part." He craved the knowledge of self and the world that comes from hardship and intense experiences. "If I can stop just one roadside bomb, it will be worth it," he thought.

His first stop was KAF. The apron of the airstrip pulsed with a crazy flock of military raptors: Predator drones, F16s, Black Hawks, Ospreys, Chinooks, Hercules and Galaxy strategic lift aircraft. Jet exhaust stung his eyes as he lugged his duffle bag toward the strange arching entrances to the Afghan terminal.

Joffre and an American colleague, Andy Golda, were directed to a pair of Chinook transport helicopters for the trip to Panjwai. The Chinooks looked like big green bananas with a rotor on the front and back. Machine guns poked out the sides and the rear gunner stood strapped on the open rear ramp, ready to return enemy fire. "I went to the Chinook on the left and Andy went to the one on the right," Joffre recalled.

Andy's Chinook was the one shot down near Panjwai in front of the Canadian policewoman and her patrol. They were part of the team that bravely and efficiently shepherded the Chinook's passengers to safety and ensured everyone made it to the base intact. A lot of the soldiers, including the major in command, had red noses and faces from flash burns resulting from the crash. "That helicopter was actually burned down to a lump of metal with ammunition cooking off," Joffre told me.

Helicopters were vital for moving between Kandahar city and Panjwai and there was initial concern that the Taliban had gotten hold of Stinger missiles left over from the 1980s. Further investigation later determined that small-arms fire brought the helicopter down, but it was pretty bad news all the same.

Joffre's Chinook was luckier and flew around the stony black mountains bulging out of the desert dust to descend safely on the landing pad behind the cement building that was the combined offices for the district government and the main Canadian base in Panjwai. Standing on top of the building like an Old Testament prophet was Haji Baran, waving and smiling. A bear of a man in a white salwar kameez, he was a former mujahideen with an angry scar on his face to show for it. The deep red gash jumped out from under his black turban, raged across the left side of his forehead and then settled down in a bushy black eyebrow. A slightly bulbous nose brooded over thick lips, often curved in a smile.

When Joffre arrived in 2010, the Taliban presence was more than military—they were introducing governance in addition to keeping up the fight. They had established a parallel legal system that included "police" who kidnapped transgressors and took them to "courts" where they were tried, sentenced and then beaten or hanged. They had shut down education, except for religious education in madrassas they controlled.

After Canada's combat responsibilities were reduced from Kandahar province to the districts of Dand and Panjwai in July,

Canadian forces were able to concentrate on Panjwai. Joffre accompanied Haji Baran to village shuras where the Taliban were watching, trying to push the writ of the government out into opposition territory. The people of Panjwai came to recognize him as a friend. One day an old farmer limped up to Joffre, reached into the pocket of his baggy pants and shyly offered a fistful of raisins from his farm. Joffre accepted the gift with a friendly smile.

"The average resident just wanted to put food on the table, and for their kids to go to school safely. Nobody wanted helicopters flying over their houses every day, or tanks rolling down the road getting into firefights with the Taliban, but privately they welcomed the presence of Canadian forces there," Joffre said.

Shuras were the connective tissue between governors and the governed. More shuras with more people meant people were moving their support from the insurgency to the government. Still, we didn't think Haji Baran was moving fast enough or aggressively enough to move the Taliban out of Panjwai. He took too long to agree to our projects and contractors, which was disrupting the rhythm of our funding cycles. We expected him to pick up the tempo.

There were rumours that he received kickbacks from contractors and harboured Taliban sympathies. When asked about this during the handover to Haji Fazluddin, he had been vehement in his denials. "I fully reject and deny these accusations that I helped the Taliban and have links with them," he said in a huff. "I did not help them—ever. Of course, if any unarmed guy comes here to my district compound office, I help them, if it's you or anyone else. Most of the people you see today in this compound have either direct or indirect links with the Taliban. I can't prevent them from coming here."

Whether or not he was colluding with the Taliban, Haji Baran was not up to the task of confronting them, extending governance and staying alive in that contested district. I think that, as a product of decades of war and an insurgency rooted in his traditional society, it was too much to expect. Behind the scenes, military decision-makers wanted a hard charger and they chose Haji Fazluddin Agha, who hated the Taliban with all his might.

Haji Fazluddin was fearless, driven by unfulfilled vengeance that was on public display. Years before, a Taliban commander had captured his son. The commander phoned him, then handed the phone to the son. As the father and son spoke, the Taliban shot him.

When Haji Fazluddin and Joffre arrived for a shura in Talukan, a remote knot of mud-walled family compounds surrounded by crazy-quilt fields of green grape vines, golden grain and bright pink opium poppies, one elder spoke up in front of his neighbours. "We appreciate the efforts that are taking place here." He was the *mirab*, the man who controls and distributes irrigation water among the farmers, a position given to the most respected member of the community. He was talking about work to restore irrigation systems to boost yields and improve roads so people could take their crops to market and get to schools and clinics. "We are in dire need of a better life here and we need more support from you," he said.

This was exactly what Joffre and Haji Fazluddin were trying to achieve—to get village leaders to show their support for the government that would bring the rest of the community along. That was the tipping point that could shift Panjwai from combat zone to development zone. It was a significant and courageous vote of confidence in the Afghan government and the Canadian troops supporting it.

The next day, that elder's body was found with a note from the Taliban. "Let this be a warning to others."

Still, the increased military presence put pressure on the Taliban. In the early summer of 2011, I encountered a Taliban commander at a gathering in the family compound of Haji Fazluddin, a ring of green-painted cement rooms surrounding a central open area where Afghan men sat on carpets and women sheltered indoors, hidden from outside eyes. Chairs were set in the dirt for the foreigners. The dusty desert, the toiling peasants in traditional dress and the earthen buildings gave an Old Testament feel to the place that contrasted sharply with the bray of our turbocharged diesel motors.

This Talib was dressed in clean new clothes, a white salwar kameez with a tidy black turban and black sandals. He had all his limbs and both eyes. His beard was groomed and his face was tanned without being weather-beaten. His expression was guarded, but glints of anger, frustration and intelligence showed through his rigid composure.

I didn't know his name but we greeted one another with courtesy. He wanted out of the fight. He was the leader of a group of some twenty fighters who were in hiding, preparing to demobilize in return for payment from the Afghan government, part of a busy effort to construct a peace of some kind. His choice to desert was surely worthy of a death sentence from the Taliban he betrayed.

"He is waiting for his payment. Even if it is less than the Taliban paid, his men want to go home," Rambo told me. He didn't get paid while I was there, and I don't know what happened to him.

In those last months before we left in the summer of 2011, the governance strategy seemed to be working. With the Taliban on their back foot, more people felt comfortable going to shuras. Haji Fazluddin sensed that the tide was turning and conducted walkabouts in towns to inspire others. "Initially we were getting maybe fifteen, twenty or thirty local elders at these weekly shuras. Over time, people started to feel safer. At one point we had too many. Over a hundred people showed up. They couldn't fit in the room," said Joffre.

Dean, working with General Habibi, put a major focus on connecting Fazluddin Agha with people in Panjwai. "We built the paved road into the horn of Panjwai through Zangabad, Talukan and Mushan. This cost money and took tons of security but it really brought the people together, as it was Haji Fazluddin's people who built the road. It boosted the economy and brought governance to his entire district."

In June, just as Joffre was leaving, Toor officially opened a government office in Bazaar-e-Panjwai, tangible proof of the progress we had made. "This was exactly what we were trying to achieve," Joffre said. "We were seeing that connection take place. It was the beginning of real governance in an area that didn't have it. One elder said to me that Panjwai had seen more development in the last ten months than in the last three hundred years. That might have been a bit of an exaggeration, but there's no doubt in my mind that progress had been felt in many areas of the district."

At least at that moment, the future seemed bright.

# Chapter Fifteen

# Clear, Hold, Build

We rolled out into the night in an armoured convoy. I poked my head and shoulders out the hatch, hands on the dark green roof of our LAV, armed soldiers in front and behind. Phil poked his head out beside me.

People in war zones develop a sixth sense about violent conflict that is latent or imminent. It could be the tension involuntarily transmitted by others around us. It might be pheromones we pick up from other people feeling the same thing. It's undefinable and different people experience in different ways. For me, the air tastes acidic.

These simple neighbourhoods no longer felt that way, thanks to simple and robust solar-powered streetlights designed by the Canadian forces. Kandahar city's electrical grid had been destroyed by decades of war. Now rows of heavy gauge steel pipes were planted in the sidewalk; bright lights perched on top switched on when the sun went down. A single solar panel charged an automotive battery that powered each light.

Darkness was a security problem and a social problem. Night gave cover to Taliban fighters planting IEDs in unpaved roads. Fighters could sneak unobserved from compound to compound through the dark, deserted streets of the city, then go home to sleep with their families. Kandaharis remained indoors, except for the rich and foreign, like those of us at the KPRT, who could afford generators and obtain the fuel to operate them.

Light changed the air. Islands of golden illumination appeared in the darkness. City blocks came alive. Little kids played tag while older sisters and brothers shushed them so they could do their homework under the lights. Women caught up on the news of who had had babies, how the children were doing at school and the price of food. Men played cards and talked politics and sports. Savoury scents of charcoal-grilled kebabs wafted from pushcarts, tempting hungry customers. Canadian armoured vehicles were familiar and not considered threatening. People went about their business without remarking on our passage down their streets.

We hoped to confer legitimacy on the mayor of Kandahar city, Ghulam Haider Hamidi, by giving him credit for the lights. He signed off on the location and timing of light installations; Canada contracted and paid for them. In this war economy, the questions of who received benefits like light, and who received contracts and profits, were of vital interest to the warlords and tribal leaders who contested power with the government. Sometimes it was a matter of life and death. We met with the mayor frequently to decide which neighbourhoods got the lights in what sequence.

Ghulam Haider Hamidi originally left Afghanistan during the time of the Russians to make a new life with his family in the US, where he went by the name Henry because it is easier for Americans to pronounce and remember. In 2006, he accepted an invitation from President Hamid Karzai to leave his job at a travel agency in Alexandria, Virginia, to become mayor of Kandahar. With his degree in finance and experience in the US, he brought an accounting lens to most things. Mayor Hamidi was the perfect candidate to install a sensible municipal administration for the half million people of Kandahar city.

Simple and frugal, Mayor Hamidi was a slight man of sixty-three years. Clean-shaven with thinning grey hair and steel-rimmed glasses, I usually saw him in a beige polyester salwar kameez. For special occasions, or in the winter, he put on a brown wool sport coat.

Mayor Hamidi's self-appointed mission was to clean up the morass of corruption in his city. In a high-pitched, nasal voice, he complained to me that, "Those prices are too high" or "That contractor is bad. This is the one you should use." Even though it was Canadian money, he cared deeply and didn't want to see unscrupulous businessmen reap unfair profits from the war economy when the money could buy more lights.

This is exactly the kind of responsible behaviour we would encourage—if we had the time. But the Canadian mission in Kandahar would be ending in a few months and it was a matter of national honour for me and my team to finish what we started. Walking away with unspent money and unfinished projects, implying that we were incapable of meeting our commitments, would have been shameful. I was frustrated with the mayor because he slowed us down. In turn, he was rarely pleased with our haste.

Mayor Hamidi's administrative frugality concealed a generous spirit and big heart. One day in March 2011, he showed up at our base unannounced with a thick bundle of banknotes in the pocket of his shalwar kameez. As he sat down at the steel table in our utilitarian conference room, Bernard Haven said, "What is that, Mayor Hamidi?"

"Oh, it's fundraising for Japan," he said. The tsunami catastrophe had just killed some twenty thousand people and was dominating world news. The mayor continued, "I have US$50,000 and I want to give it to the Japanese. How do we do that?"

It was a jaw-dropping expression of solidarity with the victims of a terrible disaster, and gratitude for the generous aid the Japanese had provided to Afghanistan. I don't know from whom he raised the money, but the message came through loud and clear: the people of Kandahar are not beggars. We advised him to go to the Japanese embassy in Kabul and give it to them. So he did. Perhaps it was unwise to walk around with US$50,000 in cash, but Mayor Hamidi wanted the Japanese to know that humanitarian values and international goodwill go both ways.

The centre of gravity in a counterinsurgency is the civilian population and whether it rejects or accepts the national government. The strategic mantra for RC South was "clear, hold, build": soldiers would clear populated areas of the enemy, hold the ground and create conditions for diplomats and aid workers to help the government of the Islamic Republic of Afghanistan improve the living conditions of its citizens. In theory, this would legitimize the government and engender loyalty. In theory, this would marginalize the Taliban. Without these social, economic and government pieces, the most we could hope to achieve was a defeated enemy brooding in a landscape of chaos and criminality. As RoCK, I tried to choose projects with a triple bottom line: beneficial for Kandaharis, supportive of military stabilization objectives and in line with CIDA's objectives.

Canada was committed to three signature projects: building fifty schools for girls and boys across the province, restoring a functioning dam and irrigation system to reinvigorate agriculture in what had been the breadbasket of the country, and the eradication of polio—Afghanistan was one of the last countries on earth plagued by that terrible virus.

The Deputy Director for Development, Barbara Hendrick, was the operational manager for our projects. Hundreds of millions of dollars flowed from Canadian taxpayers to develop Kandahar; Barb's job was to keep an eye on those dollars, make sure spending was by the book, that our projects were completed and that they delivered value for the Afghans.

Barb had been a neighbour in Chelsea, Quebec, and remained a family friend. Her daughter Krista and my daughter Jena had been friends since kindergarten. It was a wonderful surprise to see her on our team. I felt less alone. Before Afghanistan, Barb had been working in Pakistan, another hardship posting with similar development needs and security threats. She liked living and working there. Working among Pakistan's ethnic cultures, together with the inequality suffered by Pakistani women, mentally prepared her for Kandahar. What she liked best was fieldwork—trying to help everyday people where they lived. "I'm a firm believer that it's not about the money you put into the project. It's about sustainability and projects that will last because the community supports them."

Barb was always eager to get out of the compound and see everyday lives on the street. "Women doing their shopping in the little markets on the side of the street, kids swimming in some little pool of water as we passed. If you could forget for a moment that you were sitting inside an armoured vehicle, belted into a convoy, you could put a smile on your face watching the interaction of everyday people. Unfortunately, everything outside the compound had to be with military protection. I couldn't just, you know, have a meeting with the women to talk about their needs." She knew that this requirement was for her own safety, "But man, if I could have thrown off that bulletproof vest and just sat down and had a meal with them . . ."

Barb and other development staff bristled at the idea that their projects were tactics for winning the counterinsurgency. "There wasn't an appreciation for our role. We were trying to help the communities in spite of the war." Time scales conflicted. Military commanders were trained to achieve objectives as soon as possible whereas "development is a long, arduous process that doesn't happen overnight. Our project outcomes were not going to be achieved while we were there, and we knew that."

Weekly Governance, Reconstruction and Development (GRD) meetings at the governor's palace coordinated efforts with Toor's government. Toor, supported by his line directors and technical staff, chaired the meetings from the head of a four-metre-long conference table in a room with thick brick pillars. I led the side for the KPRT and our development experts. It was a formal and structured process that helped us understand the obstacles that blocked our projects and how to overcome them. As Barb said, "They were discussions of a political nature, but also about projects, about problems and solutions. Tribal structures, power dynamics, all of that stuff you can't know that until you're on the ground, living it, learning and listening to them."

As security conditions improved during the year, we took the meetings outside the governor's palace to the rural district centres, so elders could participate and see their government in action. I consider those meetings a powerful accomplishment of the KPRT.

Barb's favourite sector was education—rebuilding damaged schools and constructing new ones. "I always see schools as a lasting benefit because we laid the foundation for girls—and more children in general—to learn and become educated."

In May 2011, I accompanied Barb on a visit to our flagship school in Kandahar city, Timorshai, to see if construction was progressing as per the contract. We drove through the Kandahar city evening in a patrol of three armoured vehicles, then parked in a location that was sheltered but good for a quick getaway, if that was needed. As we approached the eight-foot concrete walls of the school compound, painted in vanilla and bright blue, soldiers from Stab A made a formation that enveloped us. Entering the playing field, soldiers took positions facing outward from the school and scanned for threats in all directions.

The workers were gone and the school was empty but nearly complete. Two symmetrical halves were stuck together like conjoined twins, with no door between them. Within the perimeter, a wall divided the two playgrounds. One side was for girls and the other side was for boys; parents would have no reason to worry about inappropriate contact.

A kind of melancholy silence drifted through the halls. We wanted to hear the click of chalk on chalkboards and children reciting lessons. Doors would open soon and students would flood in, but not until after our mission was over. Then the empty building would be a school, packed with eager students in tidy uniforms building the kind of future that can only come with education.

Sometimes education depended on the courage of the community. That's hard when it might mean placing your children and grandchildren in danger. One example was Sheikh Qalandar Primary School in the Panjwai town of Salavat. This school had been in Taliban hands but was brought under government control thanks to Canadian forces operations. It couldn't be opened until the villagers felt secure enough to send their kids there. The teachers had been intimidated and stayed away too, so the Canadian troops stationed in Panjwai provided some of its interpreters as interim teachers.

When the gates of the school were officially opened in April 2011, not one student showed up. Many of the elders, grandparents themselves, would not permit children to attend. It divided the village. The Afghan police patrolled through the village asking people to spread the news that the school was open. Residents replied that they would "get their throats cut" if they sent their children to school.

Haji Fazluddin Agha was furious. He angrily bellowed at the elders, "Get your grandchildren in school!" The direct method and strong leadership gave the people of Salavat a change of heart. The very next day, twenty-three students showed up for class. One elder even expressed an interest in having his daughters educated. Afghan courage and leadership made the difference.

The second Canadian priority, agricultural reactivation, was the responsibility of Jenny Hill, our economic development team lead. From Salt Spring Island, British Columbia, Jenny grew up in a world with "lots of hippies, peace, love and granola—and a lot of negative judgement about Canada's military engagement around the world." Her dad was a commercial fisherman, so she was used to being in an environment of working men like Camp Nathan Smith and was anxious to join the KPRT. "Kandahar was the pointy end of the stick. That appealed to me. And a huge, combined military and civilian mission was something I had never experienced before."

Jenny's previous experience had been in Africa with CIDA. Working on the Zimbabwe program as a new officer, she became discouraged with how challenging it was to effect change for everyday people when working in a country where there is a corrupt governing clique. Now she was working on a bi-national team with the massive funding Americans brought to the reconstruction of Kandahar. "My job became much broader. I was happy with it, but it was bigger than I was expecting."

The goal was to fix what had been destroyed by decades of war. "This is what usually makes the most sense, rather than trying to be wildly creative and innovative. We don't need to reinvent the wheel all the time. We needed to repair what was already there, things the people of Kandahar had been doing for centuries."

Besides improving services and boosting incomes, there was another long-term strategic benefit—jobs for young men. "These are the people most susceptible to being pulled into extremist views and terrorism. If you have an insurgency, and you are not creating positive opportunities for young men, I don't think you're going to make any change," Jenny said. One US-funded initiative involved exporting sweet melons, a traditional high-value export, to Dubai. Reintroducing melon production would increase farmer income, attract investment and eventually create an alternative to the poppies the Taliban was forcing farmers to grow.

A critical piece of the puzzle was the Kandahar business community. They were motivated by making money and, at the same time, wanted to contribute to their community. One man, Mush Khani, had a cardboard box factory and faced problems that ranged from getting cardboard and other inputs for production to generating electricity to power his machines. "Grow all you want to, but if you can't package your food and ship it somewhere, what good is that?"

Jenny brought the businesspeople together to talk with us and each other. "They were very dynamic, interesting characters. I had absolutely zero issues working as a woman and I got the sense that Afghan men had zero issues working with me. There's a certain relationship men have with each other and there's a certain way they perceive Afghan women. A Canadian woman was different. If you had something interesting to say, they wanted to hear it. I felt like I was a third gender."

Our massive investment in the agricultural sector included clearing almost fifty kilometres of irrigation canals so snowmelt from the Dahla Dam could flow across the arid landscape and crops could flourish again. These canals were of such importance to the villages and farmers of Kandahar that they were never targeted by the Taliban. But unmanaged irrigation poisons the land by depositing salts that kill crops. Jenny worked tirelessly with the vice chancellor of Kandahar University, Dr. Tawab Balakarzai, to build a soil and water lab, the only one in the country, that would serve the science, research and teaching needs of the university.

It wasn't big in the scheme of things, $3 million, but it was the kind of project that symbolized the better future for Kandahar that was coming into view. Now, for the first time, young Kandahari men and women could conduct research and complete postgraduate degrees to move their province and country forward. To give it profile, Jenny organized an opening ceremony. Behind the seating reserved for the guests of honour loomed the mosque of Kandahar University, its huge, pointed dome covered with blue ceramic tiles that mirrored the sky above. The intense cerulean reminded me of a bright spring day on the Canadian prairies.

I dressed up for the event, wearing a jacket and tie for only the third time since my arrival in Kandahar (in addition to my introductory visit with Toor, I dressed for the Remembrance Day ceremony at Camp Nathan Smith). Ambassador Bill Crosbie came from Kabul for the occasion. It was a particularly satisfying moment for Toor, seated next to me, who had been the first chancellor of Kandahar University and had dedicated his life to education.

The university laboratory was the capstone for our agricultural program. "The lab was long-term. It wasn't about winning hearts and minds so we could win the war," Jenny said. "The intention was quite pure. But also, young men needed opportunities besides fighting with the insurgents. This lab would create livelihoods that didn't involve a gun."

When the World Health Assembly launched the Global Polio Eradication Initiative in 1988, there were an estimated 350,000 cases per year in 125 countries. By 2021 there were only six reported cases around the world. The polio vaccination campaign was a huge win for humanity and a major advance for Afghanistan. The risk of new outbreaks always remained until the virus was eradicated. It still existed in Nigeria, Pakistan and Afghanistan.

As with everything else, the war made vaccination complicated, difficult and dangerous. Eradicating polio meant delivering mass oral vaccination campaigns in communities controlled by the Taliban.

The strategy rested on three pillars. The first was raising community awareness through extensive campaigns by Afghan organizations, the UN and multiple non-governmental organizations. Once mothers understood and believed this was a way to protect their children's health, the second pillar came into play. Kandahari volunteers inoculated the children, not strangers from outside the province. They knew the language, culture and lay of the land. That built trust as the campaign was repeated several times a year for successive years.

The third pillar was Days of Tranquility—an effort by the World

Health Organization and others to arrange a de facto ceasefire while thousands of volunteers fanned out across southern Afghanistan to administer drops of vaccine to newborns and children under five. The message to NATO forces and the Taliban was the same: please respect the vaccination campaign for the sake of the children. At the KPRT we communicated with the vaccination teams and connected with the Canadian forces and NATO command to advocate for Days of Tranquility.

Afghan volunteers were the foundation of the campaign and we thanked them in a message distributed through the media to all the people of Kandahar. "To the campaign volunteers, who went house to house, administering the polio vaccine to the children of Kandahar, thank you," I said during a news conference called to recognize the exceptional contributions of volunteers in Kandahar province. "Your efforts have saved lives and have helped build a brighter future for the people of this country." The brave young men and women who did the work beamed with national pride.

Impartiality of humanitarian aid is a well-established principle for ethical aid in times of conflict. The International Committee of the Red Cross (ICRC) "makes no discrimination as to nationality, race, religious beliefs, class or political opinions. It endeavours to relieve the suffering of individuals, being guided solely by their needs, and to give priority to the most urgent cases of distress." The personification of that principle in Kandahar was the remarkable Head of Public Health, Dr. Abdul Qayoom Pokhla.

Dr. Pokhla was comfortable, confident and effective in dealing with international partners. Through years of conflict, he had worked with international humanitarian agencies to keep Kandahar's Mirwais Hospital open. Smart, sophisticated and principled, he dressed in the traditional salwar kameez. His style was soft-spoken, respectful and very calm. Behind an intelligent expression, there seemed to be a deep fatigue. The years of pain and suffering endured by the people of his province, and his responsibility for their health and well-being, must have weighed on him.

Unlike other provincial department heads, Dr. Pohkla rejected the use of his Public Health department as an instrument of counterinsurgency. His over-arching priority was the health of the citizens and taking a side would not be consistent with that. He kept an arms-length distance from foreign troops and consequently enjoyed much greater freedom of movement than his peers.

Canada was a big donor to the ICRC and one of the major projects we supported was Mirwais Regional Hospital, often called the Chinese hospital because it was built with aid from China in 1979. Markus Geisser, the head of the Kandahar ICRC sub-delegation, wanted to show me, as the top Canadian representative, how Canadian taxpayer money was being used. I wanted to show my personal support, but it was standard operating procedure and a security requirement for me to travel in armoured vehicles with armed close protection and a dozen soldiers any time I stepped outside the wire. Pulling up to the hospital in a military convoy would be an egregious violation of the principle of impartiality and the ICRC's no-weapons policy. So, in December 2010, I slipped the leash.

My visit had to be secret. Nobody knew except the ICRC, Dr. Pohkla and my security detail. I didn't tell my staff and I didn't ask anybody for permission. From Camp Nathan Smith we drove in our armoured vehicles to the governor's palace. There I took off my protective gear and laid it on my seat, helmet on top. I dismounted and stepped out of the gate alone. I saw Markus and got in a soft-sided white Land Cruiser, clearly marked with the ICRC emblem.

The lightness of walking across the street without a helmet, dark glasses and heavy Kevlar body armour was liberating. With a strange irony, the weight of protective gear can make you feel more afraid. Your body carries a heavy awareness of the threat and risk that make you need protection in the first place. We drove down the road with the windows down. Fresh air cooled my face.

Mirwais Hospital was big, busy and bustling. There were patients on stretchers in hallways, but the place was better organized and cleaner than I expected. It did not appear overtaken by crisis. The atmosphere of professional dedication and competence of the Afghan and international staff was reassuring.

We visited the surgical ward. It was full of patients recovering from operations that ranged from removing bullets to removing appendices. Most had been injured in the conflict, I was told. Then we crossed over to the prosthetics workshop where Afghans were trained to make and fit new artificial legs to replace those lost to bombs and unexploded ordinance. Mirwais was a good hospital and deserved the pride that Dr. Pohkla showed when he toured me around.

While the ICRC approach to security worked in Kandahar, providing health services was initially less successful in Panjwai. In 2006, a temporary clinic set up by Canadian forces to build trust was attacked by the Taliban. Dr. Pokla also had to pull his team out of Panjwai as a result of intimidation. But by May 2011, the security situation had improved. I was with Toor and the district governor meeting with elders who now wanted health services reinstated. Dr. Pohkla was blunt as he scolded them. "Look what happened to my people the last time they came. If you want a clinic, you have to protect it. I'll consider clinics in your district on one condition. Give me a written promise that there will be no problems and put your names on it."

The next month Dr. Pokla came to the KPRT with a petition from the elders guaranteeing the security of the clinics. That paved the way for the necessary funding. By taking the clinics out of the war and connecting them directly to the community, he made them resistant to attack. They were not a target anymore.

In July 2011, the world learned of a shocking CIA plot that demonstrated the cost of violating humanitarian principles. The previous March, the CIA had recruited a Pakistani doctor to set up a fake vaccination drive to get a little blood from Osama Bin Laden's children so that they could compare it to the DNA of Bin Laden's sister (who had died in Boston) and thereby confirm his whereabouts. The doctor offered free Hepatitis B vaccines in a poor neighbourhood outside of Abbottabad, where Bin Laden was ultimately killed.

The ruse didn't work and the story broke in a report by *The Guardian*.[13] When the news hit Pakistan, villagers chased off legitimate vaccine workers, believing they were spies. The Taliban in Pakistan banned polio vaccination, citing the CIA plot. In December 2011, nine vaccine workers were murdered in Pakistan. Two months later, gunmen in Nigeria killed ten polio workers. According to Scientific American, the mistrust of vaccines caused by the CIA fake vaccine plot set back the global polio eradication campaign and may have resulted in hundreds of thousands of unnecessary deaths.[14]

Sacrificing humanitarian principles for expediency has life-or-death consequences in the real world. Adherence to them, even in hotly contested districts like Panjwai, created the minimum conditions for progress. The problems of violence, bad governance and corruption had not gone away, but we had turned a corner. Canadian development projects, big and small, enjoyed government and community support.

As Dean Milner observed, "Development and security got onside with each other. Some of the Afghans that we respected could see that things were coming along." I thought Kandahar was on the cusp of change.

13. Saeed Shah, "CIA Organised Fake Vaccination Drive to Get Osama Bin Laden's Family DNA," *The Guardian*, July 11, 2011
14. "How the CIA's Fake Vaccination Campaign Endangers Us All," *Scientific American*, May 1, 2013

# CHAPTER SIXTEEN

# BRIDGING THE GULF

With all our development team present in the conference room, I welcomed the happy occasion to hand out certificates of appreciation. Framed in dark wood, each certificate bore the crest of the Kandahar Provincial Reconstruction Team—the Canadian and Afghan flags contained within a laurel of peace composed of sheaves of wheat symbolizing the bounty of the province's agriculture—and the ISAF crest, simple white initials against a green background (green is the colour of Islam). Each certificate was signed by me as RoCK, CIDA director David Foxall and Jenny Hill.

When Jenny said with a warm smile of genuine affection, "Maryam Sahar, will you please come up," a young woman wearing a black burka of fine material with delicate blue embroidery on the hem rose from the audience and made her way to the stage. Her small shy face peered up at me from under a black shawl that modestly concealed her hair. A gentle smile graced her alert face before she composed herself into the dignified expression the occasion merited.

Stepping up to the podium for her certificate, Maryam extended her delicate hand to grasp her award as I said, "Congratulations, Maryam. Thank you for all you have done to support our mission." She thanked me and returned to the audience as others came forward for their certificates.

Maryam Sahar was Canada's first, last and only female interpreter in Kandahar. She was seventeen years old in 2011 when I presented her with that certificate.

Maryam was born under Taliban rule in February 1994. Her

father was a shopkeeper who grew grapes and pomegranates on land next to their house. The family compound that included her aunt, uncle and cousins had no electricity or running water. After her morning prayers, Maryam would fetch water from the community pump.

There was no school for her or other girls, so when she was not helping her father in the fields or her mother in the house, she played outside with her friends and cousins, searching for unspent bullets whose shiny brass shell casings made perfect play money. Other days, she and her friends would play hide-and-seek among burnt-out Soviet tanks.

"What are these things?" she asked her dad.

"You will learn when you are older," was his response.

Once she saw a metal object emerging from the shifting soil of the family fields. It was as long as Maryam's small arm, slender and very interesting. Crusted with grey corrosion from years in the ground, it was pointed at one end and a circle of sharp fins fanned around the tail. Maryam dug it out and brought it home to play with. "Look, Dad, I found a fish!" Years later, in a training course on unexploded ordinance, she learned that it was a mortar shell that could have killed her whole family.

When the family lived in Kandahar city, their home was near the stadium once used for cricket and soccer tournaments. Now, it was used by the Taliban for Friday mass prayers. Because absence could attract unwanted attention, Maryam's father always attended but without his family. "Don't let the children out of the house on Fridays," he told his wife.

Maryam was curious. So one Friday, she slipped out of the house and joined the crowd heading into the stadium.

Groups of men with big bushy beards, long hair and long robes clustered around the entrance. The Taliban attendant said to her, "Where is your stone?"

"I don't have a stone," she answered, baffled.

"Take this one."

Maryam took the fist-sized stone as if it were an entrance ticket.

Inside the stadium, a big hole had been dug in the playing field. Inside was a young woman, frantic with terror, screaming, "It's not my fault! It's not my fault!"

At the mullah's command, the men surrounding the hole started throwing their stones.

Maryam saw her dad in the stands. He rushed down to get her. Flushed with anger, he grabbed the stone from her hand, dropped it on the ground and took her, petrified and traumatized, back home.

"This is why I told you not to let her out on Fridays!" he yelled at her mother. "You know there are executions after Friday prayers." Public executions in the stadium were not infrequent, scheduled right after the Friday prayers to ensure a full house. For adultery, the penalty was stoning. For murder, the condemned would be tied to the goalpost and shot. Robbery was punished by amputation of a hand.

On a hot September night, as his family—now living in the Maiwand district outside the city—slept under mosquito nets in the front yard to escape the baked air lingering in the house, Maryam's father switched on the BBC Pashtu service and heard the first reports of the terror attack on the World Trade Center. Some nights later, the BBC reported that the Taliban governor of Kandahar had boasted that the United States would be defeated in this jihad. "The Americans will come now. Things will change for the people of Afghanistan," he said.

With ears bent to the small transistor radio every night, her father followed the progress of the war. First, the northern provinces fell to the Americans and their Afghan allies. Then Kabul fell. Kandahar would be next. Taliban leaders from Kandahar city headed east trying to escape to Quetta, Pakistan, just over the border. Commanders came through Maryam's village with the bombing campaign in hot pursuit. Maryam prayed that the Taliban would escape soon so the bombing would stop. Fear gripped the community and many families started heading for safety in Pakistan. Maryam wanted to leave too, but her father said, "We have nothing to do with the Taliban. We are not a target. As soon as things calm down, we will go back to Kandahar city. Then you will go to school."

During Ramadan of 2001, Maryam and her family huddled together in the light of a few candles placed far from windows to avoid becoming a target. The night sky flashed incandescent with a blinding white light. The accompanying shock wave thumped their house and a gust of blast wind rushed over them. She has never experienced anything that bright and that loud, before or since. It felt like the American bomb had landed right on top of them. She now thinks the target was a house of the elusive Taliban leader, Mullah Omar. It stays with her vividly.

Maryam's father had gone to the mosque to pray and find what news his neighbours might be able to share. She was certain he had been killed until he rushed back to calm his terrified family.

A few days after moving into their new house in Kandahar city, her father took Maryam and her cousins to their first school. Seven-year-old Maryam began second grade in an outdoor class with the girls sitting on the sand under the sun watching their teacher write lessons on a board stuck in the ground.

Her mornings changed. Instead of hauling water and helping in the fields, playing in burnt-out tanks and looking for bullets, Maryam would wake up, pray, have breakfast and go to school. Her father told her, "You must be one hundred percent student. Learn English and as many languages as possible. No more watching Bollywood movies on the television."

Her classmates all talked about two things. "What will we wear to school?" They had heard students would wear uniforms to school and anxiously waited to learn what colour they would be. Their second question was, "What do you want to be—lawyer or doctor?"

"I want to be a politician," Maryam said, even though her dad wanted her to be a doctor.

After the Americans drove the Taliban from Kandahar in December 2001, life for girls like Maryam changed overnight. The streets filled with life and there was a sense of joy and hope. She waved at the friendly American soldiers driving down the streets in their armoured vehicles. Fun was allowed for the first time in her life. Navroz (Afghan New Year) and Independence Day were celebrated. Music was permitted. Women walked the streets without male escorts.

With the Americans in charge, Ehsan Ullah, a Kandahari father of three daughters who had always dreamed of being a teacher, began passionately trying to bring literacy to the new post-Taliban Kandahar. Ryan Aldred, a volunteer with the Canadian International Learning Foundation, learned of his efforts through an article in the *Toronto Star* and offered to help. In 2006, they opened the Afghan–Canadian Community Centre (ACCC), with Maryam as one of its first and most enthusiastic students. English was her favourite subject; Maryam wrote poems and acted in school plays. She loved to sing, but her father admonished her to "do public speaking, not public singing." She was the speech secretary and invited local leaders to address the students.

Ehsan and Ryan brought the Southern Alberta Institute of Technology on board and the centre boomed. Over eight hundred women were enrolled. CIDA extended its funding and another thousand women were added to the program. The KPRT donated ninety computers. Soon there were hundreds of graduates taking jobs with the Afghan government, international organizations, the UN, private sector companies and government departments.

In 2009, Jess Dutton, Director of the KPRT, was invited to speak at the ACCC graduation ceremony. Security was tight. Most of the women's fathers had no idea what they were doing and they were at real risk of imprisonment or death at the hands of the Taliban. The graduation ceremony was only announced the day before. The graduating students didn't use their names. Instead they were given numbers. Jess came with enough close protection to secure the facility.

"I saw a number of the women arrive in their burqas, you know, on the back of pickups and stuff like that. Some of them spoke English quite well and I was able to engage with them. I was so inspired by these women and they were so grateful for the support that they were getting, I just threw my speech away and spoke from the heart." Jess said, "I saw lots of police stations and roads built. This was probably the first time I really saw a tangible contribution that we were making to women. It touched me deeply."

Jess sent some photos to his mother in Montreal. She wrote back and said, "Oh, I like the one with the hot pink pants." He looked at the picture again. Under the gown and the niqab, a little bit of ankle was exposed. "There was colour and vibrancy underneath."

Just as the blinding American bomb left an indelible impression, memories of that condemned woman propelled Maryam into the fight for rights for women and girls. She began volunteering at the Kandahar Women's Affairs Department where her command of English and her computer skills became indispensable to the director, Rona Tareen. Rona joked, "When I retire, Maryam, you will be running this department." Maryam was fourteen years old at the time.

The Women's Affairs Department had a problem with the Canadian forces. "These foreigners are coming to my office all the time. They are asking what they should do for women. I have so many ideas. But they just get lost," Rona told Maryam. "I need a female interpreter who believes in the rights of our women and who believes in empowerment."

With Maryam as interpreter, communication improved and more projects were approved. Then the Canadian forces reached out to Women's Affairs for assistance speaking with women all over the province.

Rona called Maryam. "The Canadians need a woman translator. It's a paying job with the KPRT."

Maryam was intrigued and excited about the possibility. "I am interested, but I need to talk to my family," she replied.

Her parents were skeptical. "You are only fifteen years old. And you look even younger than that. They will never hire you," her father said. Her mother agreed. "Have you looked in the mirror lately? You look like a child. You are a child!"

The KPRT sent a male interpreter to pick her up from her house. He took her to meet Charlotte Greenall, Warrant Officer in charge of the CIMIC (Civil-Military Cooperation) office.

"Are you American?" Maryam asked.

"No, no. I'm Canadian," she pointed to the maple leaf on her shoulder insignia. "See the flag?"

"You should tell people. I'm educated and I don't even know that the Canadians are in charge of Kandahar," said Maryam.

Maryam signed a contract for interpretation on request. It could be on the base, it could be in a district, it could be in a Kandahar government department.

When the Canadian forces went to villages, they wanted to collect information, assess the Taliban presence and open dialogue. Because men and women could not be together in these shuras, they would have a female engagement team and a male engagement team. Maryam interpreted for Charlotte on the female engagement team. While the men would meet in the district office, women would go to the home of the district leader, the only person with enough authority and security to take such a risk. Addressing a group of fifty to sixty women, Maryam asked what their problems were and what they wanted from Canada and the KPRT.

The first district women's shura was held in January 2010. Mostly the women worried about the health of their families. In the winter, cold dusty air and indoor cooking fires caused respiratory infections. Malnutrition was common. So was diarrhea from poor hygiene or dirty water in the communities. They asked for clinics, income-earning possibilities and food.

When it came to Maryam's passion, education, the women would say, "Go speak to our men, they are the ones who decide things." This pattern was repeated in other shuras.

As hard as female engagement teams tried to engage in dialogue, the results were not satisfactory. "These women did not know how to speak to us," recalled Maryam. "For most of them, this was the first time they had ever spoken with a foreign soldier. They did not know how to express their needs because they were not aware of their basic rights and they were not educated." They also did not see the Canadians as friends. "'You have killed my father. You have killed my son,' they would say. 'You have taken my man to prison and I don't even know what his crime is.' On top of that, the Taliban, who were from their culture, told them a completely different story."

During her time with the Canadian forces, Maryam was disappointed by the lack of results. Despite the needs expressed, she did not see practical projects being implemented. "We went to all these districts and we heard all these needs. But there were only a few projects, like tailoring and embroidery and some training on domestic abuse." Much later, Maryam heard that the purpose of the women's shuras was not to empower women and advance their rights, nor was it the role of the Canadian forces to promote social change in traditional villages. The shuras were primarily to collect information and better understand the districts in which the Canadian military mission was operating. "I had no idea that I was doing such a risky job."

In the summer of 2010, when Canadian forces reduced their territory, Charlotte and her CIMIC team left the KPRT. Maryam started working for CIDA, monitoring women's projects in Kandahar city and surrounding districts. She also helped the

Department of Women's Affairs develop initiatives such as selling handicrafts in conjunction with the KPRT.

Canadian civilians could not go outside the wire without a military convoy that could turn a school or clinic into a Taliban target, so Maryam travelled to the villages alone. Because she lived at home with her family and often worked with the Department of Women's Affairs, she was able to keep a low profile, travelling with a trusted driver in a motorized rickshaw that she had arranged for herself. "I would go to the village in my rickshaw, meet for two or three hours with the women, and then prepare a report." After Maryam started working with CIDA, more projects to help women were introduced.

Barb Hendrick knew from her experience in neighbouring Pakistan how hard it was and how long it took to get projects for women up and running. She had pushed for months to launch a rural midwife training program. In Kandahar, the religious and cultural barriers were exacerbated by Taliban intimidation. The only way to speak with women was with the permission of the village headman. "The men wouldn't let you near the women because they didn't know what we were going to talk about. Maybe they imagined we wanted to talk about something totally off limits, like abortion." Windows of opportunity for dialogue and trust were tiny and fleeting, but her persistence and patience ultimately paid off. The men gave permission and the project got off the ground.

Maryam particularly enjoyed the education projects, like teacher training and working with the Afghan–Canadian Community Centre school that she herself had attended. "Education was the key to empowering women so they could drive change themselves."

Maryam didn't give much thought to her own security until Rona told her that strangers had begun asking the guard at the Women's Affairs office about the interpreter who worked with the KPRT. "You need to be more careful about coming and going here," she said.

Maryam kept that information to herself. She knew if she told her father, he wouldn't let her work anymore. The next time she went to the Department of Women's Affairs, the security manager told her, "People are coming and looking for you. We have a lot of other women coming in and it's not safe for them if these suspicious men keep coming back. You need to work someplace else."

Shortly afterward, she was followed leaving Camp Nathan Smith, where she organized regular bazaars to help local women sell handicrafts to Canadians and Americans through a women's NGO. As she and the NGO's director pulled out of the gate, a white car started following them. The driver changed routes. The car kept following them. They kept driving for three hours, not wanting to give away Maryam's home address. Maryam's parents were calling her frantically. "The safest place is the Women's Affairs office," said the driver, so they went there. After a few more hours, the coast was finally clear.

The director said, "Maryam, nobody has ever followed me like this. I am a women's advocate and a member of the Provincial Council. This has never happened to me before. I think they are after you. I am not comfortable driving with you anymore, or for you to come to my organization. Tell your supervisor."

Now it wasn't just about Maryam's security, it was about the people she worked with and cared deeply about. Worried, Maryam prepared an incident report. Then her family paid the price for her work. Her twelve-year-old brother, Omer, was hauled away from the stadium where he was playing cricket with his friends and tortured for twenty-four hours.

"Who is that woman who interprets for the KPRT. Who is she?" They had seen him with Maryam but didn't know her identity.

Badly injured, Omer didn't break. "She's a neighbour. I don't know what she is doing there."

When Omer was dropped off at the family house, beaten and bloody, his head shaved by the Taliban, Maryam called her supervisor and asked for help. She and Omer got into her motorized rickshaw and were driven to the KPRT, where Omer received medical attention. He stayed at the base for a few days to recover before Maryam took him home.

Maryam's family was no longer safe in Kandahar. They moved to Kabul and Maryam moved into the safety of Camp Nathan Smith where she was given a helmet, personal protective gear and security training. There would be no more unsupervised trips in a motorized rickshaw; now she travelled in armoured vehicles.

In my thirty years of diplomacy, I came to understand that trust was our most valuable asset, that it is hard to earn and can be lost in a flash. In Kandahar, we could not understand the needs of women by asking men. The gulf that separated us from the women was vast. Our bridge across that gulf, our cultural and political liaison, was a small and slender teenager named Maryam.

# CHAPTER SEVENTEEN

# FROGS IN A POT

On July 6, only weeks before the end of the mission, I stood beside the district governor of Spin Boldak, a US colonel and Toor. Each of us was holding a shovel spray-painted gold that we would use to ceremonially break ground for the construction of a customs house that would mark the official border between Weesh (in Afghanistan) and Chaman (in Pakistan). What would be considered a prosaic event elsewhere in the world was the result of months and months of talks and visits and negotiations in Afghanistan, painstakingly arranged by the KPRT's Deputy Political Director, Greg Galligan.

Greg's job was to engage the key leaders in Kandahar, the leaders who shaped the political reality in which we worked. Within the KPRT, we had a room reserved for that purpose. The Haji Babai room, named after a Kandahar director of culture and information assassinated by the Taliban, was furnished in the Afghan style with carpets and a low table suitable for taking tea sitting on the floor.

In many countries, Afghanistan included, Canadians have a diplomatic advantage. Afghans would say, "We don't know why Canada is here." There was no conspiracy theory about a hidden Canadian agenda. "There was no sense that we were coming to take over the country to rule it or steal its resources," Greg explained. "That created an opportunity and channels for dialogue." He needed that goodwill to build foundations of trust to resolve the issue of the border, a strategic liability for the incoming US forces.

It was widely known that Taliban commanders had longstanding connections with Pakistani intelligence services that were rooted in the conflict with the Soviets. The Taliban headquarters were right across the border in Quetta, where fighters and commanders returned at the end of the fighting for rest, medical attention and further training. Although the Weesh border crossing was the outlet to the port of Karachi for landlocked Afghanistan, there was no customs infrastructure to facilitate legitimate trade and distinguish it from the thriving illicit trade in drugs and guns.

The border land was contested by two important tribes, the Achekzai and the Noorzai. The Taliban recognized the Noorzai claim while the Karzai government endorsed the Achekzai claim. And the Afghan government didn't want to compensate either party because they felt it was government land.

The American military was constantly pressuring us, relying on diplomacy, to get the negotiations completed. "The military can achieve objectives, they can secure territory, they can neutralize opposition and enemies. But it takes the diplomatic side to resolve conflict," Greg said. A challenging situation became worse in January 2011 when our Afghan government partner, Deputy Governor, Abdul Latif Ashna was assassinated by a suicide bomber who drove a motorcycle laden with explosives into his convoy. Three of his bodyguards were wounded. His death was a personal and professional blow to Greg but there was no time to mourn—he continued his work on the border project.

The assassination of Abdul Latif Ashna was the latest instance of a Taliban campaign that began shortly before I arrived as a result of a new directive issued by their leader, Mullah Omar. He had exhorted his followers to "capture and kill any Afghan who is supporting and/or working for coalition forces or the Government of the Islamic Republic of Afghanistan" and to "capture and kill any Afghan women who are helping or providing information to coalition forces."[15] This was a marked change from his previous order

---

15. Thomas Joscelyn & Bill Roggio, "Mullah Omar orders Taliban to attack civilians, Afghan women," Long War Journal, https://www.longwarjournal.org/archives/2010/07/mullah_omar_orders_t.php. Accessed May 13, 2024.

that great care must be taken to avoid civilian deaths, injuries or property damage.

The Taliban carried out his wishes with ruthless efficiency, and the United Nations reported that half the political killings in Afghanistan occurred in the southern provinces of Kandahar and Helmand. Less than two weeks after the death of Abdul Latif Ashna, they launched the attack on the Kandahar city police station that trapped the Canadian police officers. Two months after that, on April 15, a suicide bomber disguised as a police officer killed the Kandahar police chief, General Khan Mohammed Mujahid. Ten days later, the Taliban freed their fighters from Sarpoza prison.

In May, Mujahid was replaced by General Abdul Raziq. A fierce opponent of the Taliban, Raziq was young, about thirty. His face was burnt a brick red, and a habitual smile revealed a little gap between his front teeth. Until he was promoted to general, he wore the pillbox cap with a small Islamic arch-shaped opening over the forehead typical of young Afghan men. It gave him a jaunty air that belied his reputation. Prior to his appointment, Raziq had been commander of the border police in Spin Boldak, a complicated, important and lucrative job. Greg recalls that, "he had four or five cell phones all the time. They were always on the go and his hands were always moving."

Some Afghans viewed Raziq as a hero for his willingness to take on the Taliban while pushing back on Pakistani influence. He was tough and effective. He was also widely reputed to use torture and forced disappearances to get the job done.

Greg and I paid a visit to Raziq in his new capacity. Meeting in his office at police headquarters, I told him, "Canada cannot tolerate any mistreatment of prisoners. I expect you to ensure there is no torture by the police of Canadian detainees. This is of the utmost importance to Canada."

His habitual smile was missing, and his eyes held a hint of anger. He resented being lectured on how to do his job, especially as he was risking his life to serve Kandahar. As Greg said, "Raziq's under-standing of human rights was, 'Canadian prisoners get showers. They get sunlight. They don't get beaten. We're good. We're good.' By the time we were leaving, everybody in Kandahar seemed to understand that Canadian prisoners got treated well. But that wasn't rooted in any appreciation of the International Covenant on Civil and Political Rights or the universality of human dignity. It was because we said what we expected and made sure it happened."

In addition to his role as police chief, Raziq was a strongman affiliated with Ahmed Wali Karzai, the next to die. AWK was shot to death in his own home by a trusted member of his entourage, Sardar Mohammed, on July 12, 2011. Sardar was killed immedi-ately after. While the Taliban claimed responsibility, it was also possible that one of AWK's other rivals or enemies was responsible. I asked Rambo for an explanation. "May God rest him in peace. He was a big warlord in terms of smuggling, in terms of killing people, in terms of being a hitman himself. He would just call his people and tell them what to do, and who to kill. Very simple and very easy. The person who finally shot Ahmed Wali Karzai was a childhood friend. How come? How come that happens? Because he had witnessed a lot of the barbaric actions of Ahmed Wali Karzai." For all his faults, AWK had maintained a power balance between warlords, tribal leaders and the government. His death altered the balance of power, just as we were leaving.

Two weeks later, packed and ready to leave the KPRT, I was about to transmit my final report to Ottawa when a buzz of distress moved through our building—the latest anti-corruption initiative from Mayor Hamidi had gone horribly wrong. Two days previously, deter-mined to recover government land and assets that had been taken by warlords, Hamidi had ordered the demolition of approximately two hundred homes constructed on stolen land. Two children were accidentally killed by bulldozers carrying out his directive.

Mayor Hamidi did not shirk from close contact with his fellow

Kandaharis. He sought it. So, when a hundred or so protesters showed up at his office, he came out to speak with them. As he did so, a suicide bomber stepped next to him and triggered explosives hidden in his turban. The mayor's lifeless body was found next to that of the headless assassin.

It was not entirely clear who killed Ghulam Haider Hamidi. Motives for assassination were always murky and could be a blend of political, criminal and terrorist drivers. Claiming responsibility a few days later, the Taliban said Hamidi was on their hit list. But, in an interview with the BBC World Service in August, his fourth daughter, Rangina, who had originally convinced her father to go back home to Kandahar, said she thought his assassination was about money and his fight against corruption. She thought it possible that elements in the Karzai government were responsible. "They were the ones losing business in the city and they are the ones whose livelihoods depend on continuing the chaos in Afghanistan," she said. "My father was becoming a threat because he was trying to clean up and put order to the chaos."[16]

Governor Wesa said that the "housing mafia" might be happy that the mayor was dead "but we will stand and we will destroy illegal houses."

I understood that the mayor wanted to demonstrate his resolve but destroying housing in a post-conflict city seemed like a bad idea to me. By that time, I wondered if it was even possible for a leader to stay alive in Kandahar.

The litany of killings did not stop with our departure. Haji Fazluddin Agha was killed by a suicide bomber in January 2012, less than a year after taking office. Two of his sons, two police officers and a civilian were also killed. Haji Fazluddin's predecessor, Haji Baran Khaksar, was gunned down by motorcyclists in June 2014. Numerous other officials were killed in between.

Even Abdul Raziq who, in the wake of AWK's death had become

16. "An Afghan Mayor, Mourned in the US," BBC News, August 25, 2011, https://www. bbc.co.uk/news/world-us-canada-14635978. Accessed May 13, 2024.

the most powerful man in Kandahar, was not immune. After surviving numerous assassination attempts, he was shot in October 2018 as he was leaving a meeting at the governor's palace, reportedly by one of the governor's bodyguards. The head of the provincial NDS was also killed; Toor and several others were wounded.

For me, these killings evoked a strange combination of pain and denial. The victims were people I knew, with whom I had worked and with whom I shared aspirations for a better future. For all our military might, we could not protect them. There was no way to grieve with their families, or even send flowers. It would be too dangerous. For the Afghans it was worse.

At the same time, the implacable battle rhythm forced us to keep working as fast as we possibly could to meet our targets and make an honourable exit. We also needed to rapidly help the government find replacements for the victims. Like the proverbial frog in the pot, we became acclimatized to a terrifying level of ambient violence that we never took time to acknowledge. That is only visible now and from a distance in time and space.

## Chapter Eighteen

## Lowering the Flag

The ceremony of lowering the Canadian flag at Camp Nathan Smith in July 2011 was solemn and sombre. My US colleague, Ben Moeling, stood on the parade ground in front of our Canadian flag. A soft breeze gave the maple leaf a gentle flutter in the morning sunshine. At our sides were Brigadier General Dean Milner with Chief Warrant Officer Blais, and their US counterparts, Brigadier General Kenneth Dahl with Divisional Chief Sergeant Major Graca. After Dean presented the General Campaign Star to the members of the Camp Nathan Smith signals detachment in recognition of their service, the Canadian chaplain, Padre Thompson, read Palm 23, "The Lord is my Shepherd." I felt a special resonance at the words, "Even though I walk through the darkest valley, I will fear no evil . . ."

He continued, "In December 2009 we lost the following KPRT comrades: Sergeant George Miok, Sergeant Kirk Taylor, Corporal Zachery McCormack and Private Garrett William Chidley. We also remember diplomat Glyn Berry who lost his life in January 2006."

Ben Moeling spoke next. "So, I say on behalf of the many American civilians and military who have worked in this place and who have seen our two proud flags flying side by side here at Camp Nathan Smith, we have a true respect for what the Canadian flag represents and for those who stand behind it. We are grateful for your presence, we are humbled by your sacrifice, we are inspired by your accomplishments. And we are sorry to see you go. Thank you, Canada."

I concluded my remarks with what I felt and hoped in my heart,

"It is not the laying of bricks, nor the drying of mortar that we celebrate. It is what each of these buildings and projects represent—how Canadian support for the people of Kandahar has allowed them to determine their own future." I returned to my position next to Ben on the parade ground.

"O Canada" rang out of the public address system as our flag came down. It was folded into a triangle and handed to Ben as head of the KPRT. Ben gave it to Brigadier General Dahl who, with a sad smile and a word of thanks, gave it to me. I would carry the flag back to Ottawa, have it mounted in a shadow box and present it to the Minister of Foreign Affairs, John Baird.

Earlier, the US military had promised me that they would not change the name of our base—the ultimate sacrifice of Private Nathan Smith would still be honoured by the American KPRT.

On May 30, 2011, Stephen Harper had come to Kandahar to congratulate the soldiers and civilians who had served in Kandahar and to bid the troubled province farewell. I took him to the very spot that brought us to Kandahar in the first place, Tarnak Farms. It had been the headquarters of Osama Bin Laden when he planned the attacks that triggered the NATO campaign and the Canadian mission in 2001, a long ten years earlier. Tarnak Farms was where Private Nathan Smith and his comrades were killed by friendly fire. As we stood in the golden field of wheat, I pointed out the irrigation equipment from Saskatchewan that was creating this bounty, making Kandahar a breadbasket again.

The Prime Minister had decided Canada had done its share in Kandahar. More than that, the fundamental reason for going in had been satisfied. "This country does not represent a geostrategic risk to the world. It is no longer a source of global terrorism," Harper said. He added that Canada would continue to help the government of Afghanistan defend itself by leading the second-biggest military and police training mission. Our Kandahar focus was finished but the

Canadian forces would move 950 troops to a training mission run out of Kabul, along with our development program. Canada was making the second-largest troop contribution and would be there for three years.

Fatima and I listened to the speech together. She had come down from Kabul to shepherd the press as it flew by Chinook with the Prime Minister. As good as it was to have Fatima with me in KAF for a night, we could not share the same bed or room. There was still no fraternization allowed. It was a relief to know we would soon return to a normal married life together. The separation had been tough on both of us.

For us, moving would be simple: two boxes each of papers and clothes were being sent by DHL courier from Kandahar to our next posting at the Canadian Embassy in Bogota, Colombia. It was a longer process to draw down the Canadian staff of the KPRT. Vic and the bulk of civilian police had completed their rotation and left in December 2010. Other members of the Canadian team started leaving in February, unless they were engaged in absolutely essential work. Around the same time, I transferred lead responsibility for the KPRT to Ben, an energetic and politically savvy career foreign service officer, so that I could concentrate on the completion of Canada's projects.

For each and every initiative, we had a completion plan that included finishing the project, providing a formal transfer of knowledge to the US, formally handing responsibility over to Afghan authorities and ceremonially recognizing our Afghan partners, like the vaccination volunteers. Everyone had an exit interview with me. We coordinated shipping everyone's two DHL boxes home. Email accounts had to be closed and laptops returned. Then departing staff returned their helmets and flak jackets to the Canadian forces stores and got on the plane out of Kandahar. It went without a hitch except for a problem with shipping a ceremonial decommissioned land mine. As we completed the countdown, I felt my anxiety go down a notch every time someone left for KAF. We were a little less exposed.

One colleague said, "I feel mixed emotions. Joy and ecstasy." It was, of course, much more than that, but the feelings emerged slowly and needed to be processed. Marriages and children had been unattended. Lids were screwed tight on cumulative stress and repressed trauma. The physical and mental bills for Kandahar would come due later, sometimes years later.

The mission in Kandahar had been Canada's longest war, and the combat side of it, including all the attendant physical and spiritual dangers, would soon be over. I wondered if our nation would ever answer another call that took us to our absolute limits like this. Dean said, "I'm very proud of the soldiers. A lot of them went back numerous times. Canada did rise to the occasion because our soldiers could do the hard parts. They could fight the Taliban, but they also could also connect with the people and support the development. We took casualties and it was a tough situation for soldiers to keep being thrown back into that fight. We have a lot to be proud of. We fought well. We worked hard."

So had our Afghan employees. Recognizing the risks they and their families were taking for us, the Government of Canada created a program in 2009 to give permanent residence to those we thought would be in danger after we left. Other allies had similar programs. The US had established a program for Iraqi and Afghan interpreters in 2006 and the United Kingdom put a scheme in place for their Afghan interpreters to relocate in 2013.

Dean Milner and I would meet every few months to review the service record of each applicant and assess their risk of Taliban retribution upon return to normal life. Our Afghan staff who wanted to go to Canada applied with the help of the UN's International Organization of Migration. If Dean and I approved, the application would then go through immigration channels for permanent residency in Canada. A cleaner, clerk or the base barber might be ineligible, but Dean and I always recommended applicants whose jobs had put them at risk. I thought we were going to win, but we still took these decisions extremely seriously. We both felt a moral obligation to do so.

Overall, I felt good about Canada's generosity and the way the program was managed. I was dumbfounded when Rambo told me that his application, submitted before my arrival, had been refused. He had been on the front lines with Dutch and Canadian troops. He had been on TV and in newspapers with me. Rambo was a loyal and hard-working employee who had risked his life for our side. And if my interpreter was refused, it would undermine my credibility and that of the program as a whole.

Rambo would obviously be at risk in Afghanistan. I did not know it at the time, but his work had already caught up with his family. About the time his first application was submitted, night letters (*shab namaha*) started arriving. Unlike their approach to foreigners, the Taliban calibrated their intimidation tactics when it came to Afghans with family members working for us. They didn't want to push communities so hard that they lost the social acceptance that let them operate covertly. Instead of an IED, they began with night letters.

Handwritten on white paper with the signature and stamp of the local Taliban commander, the first one Rambo received said, "We know you're working for the NATO forces. Stop working there. You and your family will not like the outcome." Everybody in his village knew he worked outside and came back from time to time with money to improve the family's house, but the letter didn't say Canadian forces. So maybe the Taliban weren't sure who Rambo was working for.

Months later, the second letter came, and then a third. The fourth letter said, "If you want to stay alive and if you don't want to be harmed, tell your son to stop working for the sake of your safety. These are non-Muslims that are in Afghanistan and we are at war with them. Your son is fighting against us. We know this: that he is working in Kandahar with the Canadian forces. Stop your son from working there." That settled it. The Taliban did know what he was doing. Kandahar Taliban had been observing him and had communicated with the Taliban commander in his home village. A general threat had become acute and specific.

Rambo moved his family to Kabul. Living there was much more expensive than the village but he managed to support them with his $1,500-a-month salary. After three months, the Taliban realized Rambo's family had not stopped him from working, and that they had left the village. In retribution, "they seized all our lands, our house, everything we owned in the village," Rambo said.

He deserved to go to Canada if that is what he wanted, and I helped him with his application, which was approved this time. With that approval in his pocket, Rambo stayed on with the KPRT to the end of our mission because he liked his job. "Even though it was very risky, I loved being there and working there," he told me. With his family safe in Kabul, Rambo activated his plan to go to Canada and build a new life. He flew out of Afghanistan on May 27, 2011.

When the flag came down, I left with almost all the remaining staff. Three members of our team stayed on with the American KPRT to finish off our irrigation program and continue monitoring detainees. We couldn't walk away from that responsibility until they had all been tried and either sentenced or released.

The Taliban story was and remains enduring, whereas ours had a rapidly approaching expiry date. Once NATO decided that Afghanistan would be responsible for its own security in 2014, urgency drove us: we had to track our progress toward Afghan capability so that NATO could withdraw in good conscience. It was a technocratic, quantitative analytical process.

What else could it be when it came to drawing down a massive multilateral military operation? Each PRT in each province was given forms to fill out. "Every month NATO would send around these forms," Greg recalled. "Green, red, yellow. How close are we to accomplishing the police objective or the army one? So let's say the objective is to train five hundred riot police. Five hundred are on the payroll, so that box was coloured green. Yeah, the objective was completed. But it didn't really mean anything. It didn't communicate what was happening or where the risks were. It didn't say whether we were confident that those five hundred people would perform or could adequately manage the situation."

We had no evidence, and no way of knowing, that those quantitative numbers would have the qualitative right stuff—the courage, skill and loyalty to their leadership necessary to hang on to their country.

As things turned out, they did not.

# Chapter Nineteen

## The Fall

By August 2021, it had been six years since I left the government and all my diplomatic responsibilities. Fatima and I built a house on Pistol Lake in Minaki, Ontario. We now had more time for ourselves, our grandchildren and our aging parents. I had a consulting contract for governance advice in the Middle East to work on, and I needed to take my mom to the nursing station, but first I had some time to go fishing.

I took my rods, some minnows and a coffee down to the dock and cast off. My little boat sliced through the calm water and headed ten kilometres north to some underwater reefs I thought would be good for pickerel. Quietly trolling among islands of bare granite and majestic white pines, I picked up a few keepers and then headed home.

Sipping black coffee out of the same stainless steel mug I used in Kandahar, I tapped my iPhone for the BBC World News podcast. The lead story was the chaotic fall of Kabul. In haste and humiliation, citizens and embassy staff of Canada, the US and other allies had barely escaped. My heart sank. The capital of Afghanistan had fallen to the Taliban without a fight.

Had it all been a fool's errand?

Phil Lupul has a unique perspective because he had remained in Kandahar to continue the detainee monitoring program after the rest of us left, embedded with the US operations that had taken over Camp Nathan Smith. He then served in the Canadian Embassy in

Kabul where, like everyone else, he saw security deteriorate as the Taliban launched terror attacks on the international presence.

The trend was becoming clear when Bernard Haven returned to Afghanistan in 2017 with the World Bank. "What you saw in Kabul in the years that followed 2011 was a shrinking bubble. The suicide bomb threat was huge. One went off outside the German embassy. The blast wave knocked out our windows and ceilings. Very, very frightening." The Taliban were advancing on the provincial capitals and were able to mount attacks on ministries, diplomatic quarters and UN agencies in Kabul.

He described an attack on a ministry that almost killed his colleagues. It was a typical Taliban operation: first, suicide bombers dressed as Afghan police entered and tried to shoot everybody; when the real police arrived, the Taliban exploded their suicide vests; more Taliban were waiting outside to ambush the next responders.

At the onset of the attack, international staff ran to the safe room. After an initial all-clear was sounded, they made their way to an armoured vehicle. "Not all the insurgents had been killed. The staff remained trapped in this car for hours as gunfire continued around them. This was happening in Kabul, but it felt like Kandahar."

The way the Taliban took over, without serious resistance from the Afghan police and army, angers Joe McAllister. Even though his resources were limited and unequal to the challenge of building a police force in Kandahar, he maintains, "We provided good information, good training. We did solid work." Joe's voice is assured, low and a little gravelly. "I am a little bit mad at the Afghan men, all the soldiers and police officers that we trained. They wouldn't stand up and fight for their mothers and their daughters and their wives and their sisters. I'm mad at them. But I don't feel it was our fault."

I thought we should have stayed at the KPRT longer. The Americans asked us to stay longer. The head of the US team there told me the US government wanted Canada to stay. I relayed this request, but the decision had been made. The Government of Canada had given as much as it thought the people of Canada had to give.

Barb Hendrick still remembers the day she turned off the lights. "I was the last one out of our development office and I thought, 'I'm one of the fortunate ones. I get to go home.' But that struggle for the Afghans is going to continue." She understood why we had to leave, but she took it personally and felt guilty for abandoning the people of Kandahar.

It is inevitable that Barb and others felt that we were leaving too soon. We had planted seeds that take years to germinate, grow and bear fruit. "I understood that we had to leave because the military was leaving. It's just the way it works. Did I feel we were leaving too soon? Yes. I didn't like the fact that we were answerable to the military—that they were holding the strings. And if they pulled, we had to come. I didn't like that at all, because I think we could have done more, but we couldn't have done it without military protection."

Immediately after Kabul fell, I tried to reach my interpreters, knowing that they would be subject to reprisal, and maybe assassination by the Taliban. I used Facebook to get the word out that I wanted to contact Rambo to see if he was okay.

On August 13, 2021, I received a Facebook messenger text: "Hello sir, this is Ahmad Shoaib, AKA Rambo." It was the first time I heard his real name. Now that we were in touch, I learned what had happened to him since leaving the KPRT.

As Rambo was preparing to leave for Canada in 2011, his mother said, "I want to find a girl for you and get you engaged."

"No, Ma," he had replied. "It's too soon. I need more education and a job. Let me see how it goes. I don't want my bride to struggle in Canada."

Rambo had been right. It was not easy. The Government of Canada provided "some money for the first year and some basic needs for our kitchen, living room and bedroom" but he was on his own when it came to education and finding a job.

Having worked for Foreign Affairs in Kandahar, Rambo decided to study political science at York University. He had unique experience working with Canada's team in the epicentre of the first geopolitical crisis of the twenty-first century, his Canadian colleagues gave him good references and he reasonably thought it could lead to a rewarding career in diplomacy.

It was a mistake. He was surrounded by immature and naive undergraduate students and, with Canada's focus shifting away from Afghanistan, there were no jobs in Foreign Affairs available to him. He decided to take a more pragmatic approach and enrolled in George Brown College to become a Master Electrician while his mother found a bride for him.

Kabul had been getting steadily more dangerous, so when he returned to marry, it was safer to hold the marriage and wedding party across the border in Peshawar, Pakistan. Despite his college diploma and permanent job, marriage to Rambo did not automatically secure a visa for his wife. She couldn't even visit. She would have to wait for her visa to be processed before she could enter Canada.

For the next couple of years, the couple waited for the all-important visa so they could set up their household in Toronto and start a family. Frustration turned to panic when, on August 12, 2021, he opened Twitter and learned that President Ashraf Ghani had fled Afghanistan and the government had fallen. The Taliban enemy was now in charge of the whole country.

He immediately called his family. Through tears, his mother said, "The Taliban are driving around! They are everywhere in Kabul city!"

Rambo was desperate to get his family out of danger and bring them to Canada. But to do so, the family needed to apply for passports, which meant providing all their information to the Taliban government. When his brother went to the Afghan Interior Ministry, he was detained for two days of interrogation and beatings.

When Rambo heard that, he told his brother, "Just leave everything behind. Your life and safety are more precious." His brother and family illegally crossed into Pakistan and took refuge in Peshawar. They were safe from the Taliban, but they were vulnerable to being picked up by the Pakistani police and deported for illegal entry. If they were caught after a second illegal entry, it would mean years of jail time. So, despite the dangers, his family returned to Afghanistan for Pakistani visas. I did what I could to help, writing letters of support and connecting with our immigration officials in Canada and Pakistan. It took multiple attempts, thousands of dollars and untold stress, but they were ultimately successful.

Rambo is a Canadian citizen now and works as a master electrician in Toronto. He and his wife have two sons, Sami and Salar. To advocate for other interpreters who faced the same agonizing situation, Rambo heads up an association of Afghan interpreters pressing for more government action to bring their family members to safety in Canada.

Like Rambo and our other interpreters, Maryam applied to go to Canada and arrived in October 2011. She continued her education and received a master's degree in Migration and Diaspora Studies from Carleton University.

Maryam's school has managed to survive in Kandahar. It is now called The Kandahar Institute for Modern Studies. The former director, Ehsan Ullah, told me, "The school is open. Currently there are more than 200 girls enrolled and attending their classes regularly both online and physical classrooms." Ehsan is now in Canada, working multiple jobs, and helping to keep the school going.

Dean is angry about the situation in Afghanistan. "The world should not have left. It's a mess now. I think terrorism may jump back in there. The Taliban are mucking everything up. And these Afghan interpreters and soldiers worked alongside us. They fought alongside us. They were killed alongside us. We should be doing everything in our power to be vetting and bringing them out and doing more than we're doing right now.

"I am still working my butt off, dealing with a very bureaucratic, not very interested IRCC (Immigration, Refugees and Citizenship Canada). I've got Afghans at the Canadian Embassy in Pakistan who can't finish their paperwork. They are getting zero responses. It's asinine. It's pathetic. I've got so many bad words to say. Sure, we're going to bring in some Ukrainians. I mean I'm okay with that, but we have a lot more Afghans that we should be bringing in. We should be making things more streamlined, less bureaucratic. And I one hundred percent support bringing them in."

Major General Ahmad Habibi and his family also fled Kabul when it fell to the Taliban. He worked with all Canadian commanders in Kandahar during the five-year mission. He speaks with respect and admiration for the Canadians he worked with. His first Operational Mentor and Liaison Team was led by the current Canadian Chief of Staff, General Wayne Eyre, and it shaped the future role of the 1st Brigade in Kandahar. Habibi conducted operations with Canada especially in Zhari, Dand and Panjwai districts. Like Dean, he speaks with special pride of the roads and schools built. "The Canadians in Kandahar were successful in the training of the National Army and the National Police, operations to eliminate the enemy and in reconstruction work. General Dean Milner is a brave general, kind to the people, and a good leader. The Afghan security forces have special respect for him as the commander who was able to complete the Canadian operations in Dand and Panjwai districts of Kandahar province, and then responsibly hand over to the Afghan security forces and the US when his job was done."

Habibi lives outside of Toronto now. When I interviewed him, he was wearing jeans and a navy blue Tommy Hilfiger polo shirt. A hard and dangerous life has not lined his broad face with premature years. Dark eyes flash over a hawklike nose with a keen intelligence his limited English struggles to express. As with many Afghans, his courage wears a smile.

Dean said, "Habibi is somebody I'll never forget because, you know, he got it. He gave it his all. He was a leader who was out there on the ground, training his guys. He was well-respected in the community. he was somebody, I think, who really understood the fight, understood working with Canadians and Americans." Habibi was awarded the Canadian Meritorious Service Medal for his contribution to the Canadian mission and forging an enduring bond between the Afghan National Army and the Canadian forces.

A Canadian citizen, former Kandahar governor Tooryalai Wesa was able to leave Afghanistan without incident before it fell to the Taliban. Driving to his quiet, middle-class neighbourhood in the Vancouver suburb of Coquitlam, I looked down from the heights of enormous steel bridges to the waters of the Fraser River. The snow-capped coastal mountain range rose to the north.

From the outside, Toor's two-storey grey stucco house is not very different from others in the neighbourhood, some growing old more gracefully than others. A little bit of the Afghan taste and style comes through in the tall pillars of the front porch and the ornate chairs in the receiving room where the Wesas graciously welcome their guests. In the place of honour, on the mantle toward which the room is oriented, Toor has carefully placed the graduation pictures of his three daughters. Mina is a physician, Hila is a lawyer and Wazhma is a business executive. His wife, Rangina, is a medical doctor with a specialty in gynecology.

Toor is the Afghan leader with whom I worked most directly and he greeted me with a friendly handshake. He took a brocaded armchair; I sat across from him on a similarly upholstered couch. Now a trim and healthy seventy-year-old who walks ten kilometres a day, he has grown a short beard that, like his hair, is salt and pepper. He speaks softly, with the calm assurance and demeanour of someone who has a clear sense of right, wrong and duty. Looking back, he remains proud of what he accomplished during his time as governor.

International resolve to rebuild Afghanistan gave way to fatigue and then resignation. President Donald Trump promised to pull US troops out of Afghanistan on October 8, 2020. Trump authorized the negotiation of a peace agreement between the United States and the Taliban and, after hasty negotiations that excluded the government and people of Afghanistan, the deal was signed. It is officially entitled "Agreement for Bringing Peace to Afghanistan between the Islamic Emirate of Afghanistan which is not recognized by the United States as a state and is known as the Taliban and the United States of America."

It is a terrible agreement. The only commitment required of the Taliban was not to allow on the soil of Afghanistan "any group or individual against the security of the United States and its allies" in exchange for the "withdrawal of all foreign forces." The words "rights" and "women" do not appear anywhere in the agreement. Nor did the agreement provide any protection against reprisals for the Afghans who worked with us.

The writing was on the wall. What the international community had constructed could not be sustained. One Afghan province fell after another. As the circle around the capital of Kabul closed, the Canadian Embassy ceased operations on August 15, 2021. The Canadian forces sent transport planes and personnel, including special forces, back to Afghanistan to help with the evacuation of Canadians, Afghan embassy staff and others. Thirty-seven hundred people were evacuated. Canada committed to accept 40,000 Afghan refugees and met that commitment in October 2023.

Over the course of a twenty-year war, the Taliban prevailed over the combined resources of NATO.

# CHAPTER TWENTY

# JUST ANOTHER FOREIGN FORCE

When our mission was over, my staff and I all rushed off to our next assignments without taking the time to internalize and digest the most intense experience of our professional lives. In the thirteen years since I left Kandahar, I have come to realize how much I didn't understand about the place. Interviewing former colleagues has given me a better understanding by situating our mission in a broader timeframe, one that includes the catastrophic fall of the country to the Taliban. There is not one Kandahar experience. Everyone who served had a unique and complex perspective, and different lessons they carried forward into their professional and personal lives.

Greg Galligan was Canada's Ambassador in Bagdad when I spoke with him. "An effective diplomat," he says, "has the ability to listen and understand. Canadians have a diplomatic advantage in many countries." Applying that to Kandahar, Greg said, "We seemed to enjoy a more positive reputation than other countries that were there. And some of that is perception. Some of it was conduct. Some of it is history. We kind of fit."

Looking at the ultimate outcome, Greg faces the fundamental question head-on. "Was it worth it? I would say, of course it was. We achieved what we needed to. The United States had been attacked and we went to demonstrate that we were a reliable NATO ally. And in that sense, we achieved our objective. We went. We did the hardest job possible. We did it for years."

Dr. Howard Coombs, our former counterinsurgency advisor,

says, "Canada's mission evolved in a way that nobody would have expected in the early 2000s." A soldier–scholar, Howard now teaches advanced military studies at the Royal Military College in Kingston. "The biggest threat in 2004 was warlordism—power brokers who wanted to inject themselves into the government process. Fast forward and we were fighting a war, a full-fledged war."

Dean Milner agrees. "This was our first really honest, full-fledged counterinsurgency fight," said the general. A big man who looks, moves and talks like a CFL quarterback, he was wearing a Winnipeg Blue Bombers hoodie when we talked. "The biggest challenge, I think, was the ratio of troops that you needed on the ground to fight a counterinsurgency."

Dean believes peacekeeping still has a place in the world, but it is becoming less relevant, freezing conflicts instead of solving them. "There is a comfortable idea out there that peacekeeping is more virtuous than combat. But to be a good peacekeeping force, you also need to be able to peace-make." With characteristic bluntness, he says, "You need to be able to war-fight first, because peacekeeping can go ugly. You need to be robust. You need to be capable. You need to have a strong enough force to deter both sides from going back at it."

He worries that we don't have the military we need. "I think the world's more complicated right now and this country needs to focus on the bigger things—being prepared to war-fight, being prepared to deter other countries. We are not deterring anybody right now. They've let us get so tiny and we're not equipped. Canada's not taking the lead. We're becoming bystanders. We're riding the coattails of other countries. I could go on and on and on. I'm just not happy.

"We had a huge impact in Afghanistan," Dean maintains. "We developed counterinsurgency capability. We learned a lot in Kandahar and I'm very proud of that." He also believes that working with the combined capabilities of the federal government and linking security to development is a fundamental capability for a new era. "The whole-of-government piece is very important."

The value of an integrated approach also struck Phil Lupul. Casually dressed, his thick black hair combed straight back, Phil spoke to me from the balcony outside in his apartment in Khartoum, Sudan, where he was the Canadian Ambassador. It was another war-torn country, on the verge of collapsing back into a genocidal civil war. Another country where deadly conflict is normal. His strong jaw signals his determination to get real things done. "In retrospect, it's absolutely clear to me that if you go into this sort of conflict without the civilian capacity to complement the military side, you've only got half the equation there. Ultimately, it's about trying to build a credible government that the local population can identify with and have confidence in."

If our approach to war and peacekeeping evolved, our objectives did not. Howard thinks that we had an unrealistic definition of success. "We are hidebound by our visions of what victory looks like. And in many cases, we default to this very Napoleonic vision of decisive victory. Napoleon won wars by defeating the enemy's field army. Or by occupying the capital city. Or doing both things. Even today, we unconsciously think of victory in that fashion."

He believes that a kind of peace could have been negotiated in 2011 during the last year of the Canadian combat mission, when the Taliban were feeling the pressure and the Kandaharis were starting to see and feel the presence of their government. "At the end of the day, we just didn't recognize the fact that, like a used car salesman, we needed to strike a bargain. It might not have been completely satisfying to us but it wouldn't have been completely satisfying to them either. We kept seeking that decisive ultimate victory with the unconditional surrender kind of outcome. And we never got there."

Mike Detroit agrees the war could have ended much sooner and in a much better way. "I personally think Afghanistan was lost in 2003 or 2004 when the Taliban didn't want to fight anymore.

Everybody was ready to stop fighting and go back to their fields. Instead of letting them be, American Special Forces, Canadian Special Forces, British Special Forces just decided to kill them or send them to Guantanamo." The missed opportunity makes him angry and he speaks with passion. "At one point they realized we weren't going to leave them alone. So they thought, 'They wanna dance? Okay, we're going to dance with them.'"

Mike believes NATO's vast resources and choices of partners encouraged corruption, something that also struck Ben Rowswell. Ben is fit and youthful, though flecks of grey are creeping into his light brown hair. When his face opens into a friendly smile, there is a small gap in his front teeth. He had been ambitious and successful as a single diplomat in hard places, and then he met the love of his life in Afghanistan. When I interviewed him, he had left the government and was working on human rights issues related to First Nations communities. Speaking with clarity, intelligence and regret, Ben said, "My biggest challenge was coming to terms with the power of Ahmed Wali Karzai, and the corrosive influence he and the power brokers had on the government that we were there to support. Ultimately, I believe, that sowed the seeds of failure of the entire mission."

"Sometimes, I had the sense of being in a gangland war," Phil said. "Each side, you know, knocking off the other. And that's just the way it was. I don't think we really understood the complexity of what was going on there and what was at stake for the Afghans we worked with."

As the District Stabilization Officer in Panjwai, Joffre LeBlanc worked with local power brokers on a daily basis. Thirteen years later, he is a Deputy Director for Defence and Security Relations with Asia. His fine features are sharp and his alert brown eyes are piercing, even when he is relaxed. "It is tragic in many ways and heartbreaking when you look at it, looking back on the outcomes. But, you know, nothing is ever guaranteed in these types of environments. Afghanistan is one of those places that requires generations of massive amounts of support. It's a tough call, to sustain that kind of effort."

For Collin Goodlet, our former Chief of Political Intelligence, power brokers were both cause and consequence. "That's just what happens when the government can't give you what you need to get by. There is a big void to be filled and power brokers come in where the state is absent. And they exact a price for that service. But there's a desire by all of humanity to be reassured someone is out there who will protect you and give you what you need to survive." His quick smile transformed his face. "When your necessities are provided for, you will compromise on a lot of political choices."

A worldly and progressive Afghan who believes in democracy for his country and education for both men and women, Rambo sees the war as a contest between good leaders and the warlords. "There were educated people with pure hearts," Rambo says, "but at the same time, war profiteers created companies for large international military contracts. Power brokers made huge profits and fostered a business culture of corruption that took root." He thinks that Canada was mostly working with the right leaders, but the mission failed because those leaders did not have enough power and influence. Speaking from Canada, Rambo shared observations he kept to himself in Afghanistan. "Even though the Canadian government invested a lot of money in Afghanistan, the people the Canadian government trusted . . . some of them were corrupt."

Adam Sweet, one of our communication officers, thinks polarized domestic politics clouded the mission. "Part of the challenge was that the Afghanistan mission became synonymous with George Bush. In Canada, the war was synonymous with Stephen Harper. The Afghan mission was painted as a right-wing conservative neocon thing, bringing democracy etc. instead of the actual work on the ground of helping people rebuild after decades of war. The minority government through to 2011 also meant that any issue that hurt the government, no matter how small or how irrelevant to the reality on the ground, was going to be front and centre for weeks and months on end in Ottawa, instead of actually dealing with the goddamn stuff that kept people alive."

When I saw Bernard Haven on Google Meet, he was in his apartment in Dhaka, Bangladesh. "Very intelligent people of good-will were coming up with our plans for Kandahar," I began. "People like you. How come it didn't work?"

A tall, slender young man with dark hair, Bernard's voice sounds like a clarinet playing classical music. "There was so much power," he said. "Think about it. When we landed in Kandahar, the Afghans had no control. We didn't go through any Afghan immigration control. They had no idea who was coming into the country. You just disembarked and proceeded to your command unit."

I knew what he meant. The military reality we stepped into at KAF totally dominated the Afghan reality. The violence distorted normal human relations between Afghans and Canadians and limited opportunities to go outside the wire to observe the Kandahari reality directly. Military plans, made in good faith and on the basis of the freshest and best intelligence, crowded out other aspects of the planning process.

Bernard found it disturbing that this organizational machine had the power to shape perceived reality. "You make plans. Those plans dictate what the reality is going to be. You declare it to be so, and then you try and enforce it." He recovered his sense of humour and an ironic chuckle slipped out. "What was very difficult as a civilian was the idea that the military was conducting psychological operations." He was referring to influence operations to get the Afghans to believe in the storyline we needed. "They call it PSYOPS, which often comprised crude, unconvincing propaganda to shape public perceptions."

He got serious again. "The primary PSYOPS was internal," Bernard said. "Truths were not being communicated accurately.

I think we also fell prey to that misinformation a lot at the time because it was very difficult to know what reality was. We weren't speaking to regular people with any frequency. We were convincing ourselves about the state of the world and how things were." Bernard and I had looked at the same things when we worked together in 2010 and 2011. Talking to him these many years later, I realized that he saw them with a healthy dose of skepticism. I had thought we were on the right track. Bernard had not.

Terry Hackett, responsible for reforming Kandahar prisons, now heads up the global work of the ICRC on the protection of detainees from their headquarters in Geneva. "Kandahar changed everything about every aspect of who I am today. It opened my eyes to the larger world. If you take away somebody's dignity, you lose your own humanity. And this was the message that we would try to pass on, to exercise safe, secure, humane control over detainees or inmates. It is much more effective to do it while maintaining their dignity. It has a moral impact on you as well."

Kandahar made Terry realize that he wanted to contribute to bringing humanity and dignity to the way we approach detainees. He resigned from Correctional Service Canada as a senior executive at forty-two. "It shocked everyone, but I landed on my feet. Kandahar sent me in a completely different trajectory. To me, it was much more about seeking to contribute or even seeking redemption for the fact that perhaps we did not make a difference in Kandahar."

I asked Terry if the Kandahar mission was worth it. "One of the first things I learned there is that you have to be proud of what you accomplished in the moment. You can't look ten years out. You can't look five years out. You sometimes can't look a week out. If, during that day, you're able to get across the message so one person sees detainees as human beings, fellow Afghans and people for whom they have a duty of care, you can be proud of the job you did."

Jenny Hill also learned to celebrate small victories. A power-house in a petite package—independent-minded, determined and fun—Jenny has been an ambassador (to South Sudan) and senior official with Global Affairs. Her views on development assistance are tempered by the searing reality of the Kandahar experience. "I sort of got over my belief that development was actually going to change anything. But if, for a certain amount of time, in a particular location, we made some people's lives better, I think that's okay. That's not a bad outcome."

Our aid was a gesture of generosity and goodwill from a fortunate country to one in deep distress. Jenny doesn't think more money would have made a difference. Afghans and Canadians were risking and losing their lives and doing their very best but our development projects were not—and could not have been—agents of structural or systemic change. That had to come from the government and the people of Afghanistan.

Bushra Saeed-Khan, who paid such an enormous personal price, felt and still feels that Kandahar shifted the attitude of Canada in a good direction, that it matured views about Muslims after the terrorist attacks on New York and the Pentagon. Crude generalizations about Muslims were gradually replaced with an understanding that Afghans mostly wanted a safe home with food on the table for their families. "So that was really nice to see because right after 9/11 there was so much Islamophobia and racism. Even despite these very difficult circumstances, it felt like we were engaged in a worthwhile cause."

Ottawa was experiencing a heat wave when we met on Zoom. Bushra is very youthful, so the couple of grey hairs starting to appear in her pulled-back black hair were a surprising intrusion. She wore a long-sleeved T-shirt with a modest scoop neck. Penetrating dark eyes looked at me through round glasses with oversized black frames. "I remember speaking to my dad after I was back in Canada. In his opinion, the entire war was for women. He said, 'Let's be honest, the war is to help the women become equal in society.' And that's how he viewed it."

It is impossible to overstate the gravity of the painful injuries Bushra sustained to her body, brain and psyche as a result of that IED. She spent an excruciating year and a half as an inpatient in the Ottawa Hospital, underwent multiple surgeries, together with intensive physical and mental therapy. Bushra continued as an in- and outpatient for months more. Her family was her source of strength. "I always say my parents raised me twice. They took care of me when I couldn't take care of myself as a child and as an adult. After this injury, when I became a child again, I needed to be spoon-fed and needed to be bathed. My mom slept by my bedside every night for at least three or four months."

Now Bushra walks with a prosthetic leg. She has resumed her career and works at the Canadian mission to the United Nations in New York, working for peace and security at the premier address for global diplomacy. She is still very careful about how she describes her experience. "It's overwhelming for me sometimes," she said. "Right now, I'm still processing these things. I don't have set talking points or set perspectives, and I find it changes every few years. When I was twenty-five, I just wanted to be involved. Now that I've become a mother, I hate to admit it, but my worldview has changed. And I'm sure in another five years I'll have a completely different opinion."

For me, Bushra exemplifies three kinds of courage: the courage to take her skills and serve the Canadian mission in Kandahar, the courage to overcome her devastating injuries, and the courage to embrace life again and start a beautiful family.

Parenthood has also changed Collin's perspective. When I interviewed him, he was at his home in Ottawa on paternity leave with his new baby girl. "This is an odd thing to say," he told me, "but my experience in Afghanistan really taught me how I should be a parent. Kids have to take some risks. And sometimes the kids fall flat on their faces. Things don't always work the way you want."

A pre-deployment requirement for young officers like Collin was a last will and testament, something most people in their twenties don't think about very much, and not a normal condition of employment. Along with his will, Collin wrote a message to himself setting out the reasons that he decided to go to Kandahar to help him get through the hardship and distance from loved ones, or when he thought about his friends in Canada going to the bar for a drink and a laugh. More importantly, in case he was injured, or worse, he and his loved ones would have a record of how he had justified his choice.

He didn't tell me exactly what he had written. "I think I looked at it from a very grandiose level. It was an opportunity to participate in a global event where Canada had an influential role and impact on the ground. That doesn't happen very much on the world scene. And I wanted to explore the human condition, like what motivates people to go to war. I had always thought war was an immature way to settle conflicts. Now I know what a naive view I had."

We were offering aid and security to Afghans, compared to the benighted cruelty of the Taliban. We were telling a story of valour, generosity and the virtue of our purpose. It was a true story and we should be proud of it, but the Taliban were telling a better story about Islam, which literally means submission to God. Islam is at the core of Afghan identity—an anchor for both pride and shame that defines what it means to be a good person and lead a virtuous life.

Collin has thought a lot about this question. "Humans are always looking to be part of something bigger than themselves. And when you elevate that to a religious story and you have religious scholars and religious schools repeating the message, it is very hard to import Western views of good governance and human rights." With help from ultra-conservative circles, the Taliban appropriated the sole authority for the interpretation and enforcement of Islam and welded it onto Pashtun culture and values, then moved beyond the realm of personal religious choice to form a coercive government.

Most members of the KPRT experienced a feeling of solitary disorientation upon returning to Canada. Their work in Kandahar was hugely consequential and they had risked their lives to do it. But back in Canada, their contribution went unrecognized. After three years in Afghanistan helping NATO shape the Afghan police institution, Joe McAllister realized, "The rest of the world really doesn't give a shit about some of these places. It's not their problem, so why should they worry about it?"

What Joe remembers most are the ramp ceremonies. "Watching those coffins go into the transport planes. But also seeing their buddies, the ones who'd been injured in the same attack, in wheelchairs or on crutches, watching their comrades placed in the hold of the aircraft, then seeing those young boys cry. Those kids were younger than mine."

The lack of acknowledgement led to resentment and an unhealthy withdrawal from society. "It took me a while to get back into being the social person I like to be. I came to understand that people didn't understand me because they didn't have those experiences." Joe used his experience in Kandahar to help NATO draw up blueprints for future policing missions. Now he is chief of security for the Canadian Red Cross and has been travelling to Ukraine to help keep humanitarian workers safe.

Adam had a similar experience. "We came back changed, but our friends and family hadn't. The only ones you can share with are others who experienced mental health challenges or critical incidents. They understand the hurt and the passion and intensity of Kandahar." After their return to Ottawa, Adam's friendship with Katherine Heath-Eves became something much more. Married now, they live with their son, Jack, in Edmonton.

The floodgates of memory and survivor guilt opened for Adam on Remembrance Day 2022, when he attended the ceremony to honour Corporal Zachary McCormack, who grew up near his Edmonton home. Zachary had been on LAV Charlie with Michelle, Bushra and Kirk, the one Adam was supposed to be on.

Coming home was also very difficult for Terry. He had to process the losses of people he worked with and the loss of friends and colleagues from the Canadian forces. He had to come to terms with the chances he and his team took. "This was hard on my family. It was definitely hard on my wife and daughters." Coming home meant coming down to a new reality. "From the Governor General to the Prime Minister—everyone came out to see us. The next thing you know you are dealing with a broken furnace. It's hard to go from one extreme to the other."

Vic Park found he could not relax and couldn't share how he felt. "My body was wrapped up beyond control for six months. I had lots of stories to tell, but all your coworkers and neighbours don't want to hear them. They treat you like another person who walked away from their job and left the slack for somebody else to pick up. That disturbed me."

The only people who understood him were veterans. He went to the Legion in Ottawa and gave a presentation on the role of the Mounties in Kandahar. One hundred people came. At the end of the presentation, Vic got a standing ovation. "Those people really understood what I had gone through." Vic sought counselling and was diagnosed with PTSD, for which he is still in treatment. He is getting his life back in order now. "There's not a day goes by in my life that I don't think of Kandahar. The good, the bad and the ugly."

Barb Hendrick learned a lot about herself during her time in Kandahar. Tall and slender, Barb grew up on a farm, used to the hard work and patience that goes with development. "I realized I was more resilient and perhaps stronger than I thought I was. And although it was tough, it didn't dampen my passion for development work." While we can't know what remains of the projects Barb and her colleagues completed, she is proud of her work and believes development was the right thing for Canada to do. "People needed our help. And they deserved it."

Despite her calm demeanour and ready smile, hearing people complain about inconsequential things or minor inconveniences makes her irritated at times in a way they had not been before she went to Afghanistan. "To be fair however, I can't expect people to understand how I feel unless they have lived those same experiences. I'm very grateful for what I have and I don't take things for granted. My Kandahar experience increased that ten-fold."

Kandahar also gave Barb a new respect for Canada's military. She appreciated the protection they gave her and grieves the soldiers we lost. "That alone left me changed." It had a similar impact on Jenny. Working closely with the Canadian forces and getting to know individual soldiers gave her great respect for our military. A curious person, every time she got into an armoured vehicle with soldiers she would ask, "Why did you join the military?" She quickly realized that her negative preconceptions were based on a complete lack of information. She learned that the soldiers were motivated by a strong sense of public service and patriotism that she had never seen before. "For many, it was a matter of honouring a family tradition. Their mother or father had been in the military."

Jenny's outlook on the duty of care owed to Canadians serving in conflict zones also shifted. "The Afghanistan experience taught me to practise duty of care as a core responsibility. The Canadian government started taking it seriously for civilians in Afghanistan especially after Glyn Berry was killed, but it took some time for this to extend to other dangerous places."

She observed that working in insecure environments impacts people differently and now makes duty of care a priority, whether it is approving travel for staff or thinking through crisis management plans. At the same time, she does not mind taking those risks for herself. "It's probably a maladaptive evolutionary behaviour, but I didn't feel daily stress around an attack even though I knew the potential was obviously there given how many people we knew that were injured or killed. If anything, the insecurity made it harder to leave. I felt like it was too soon and more needed to be accomplished, especially because so many had suffered."

Maladaptive or not, ignoring personal danger was common among KPRT members. Glyn Berry went to Kandahar because he thought that the Afghans deserved a better life, and the Canadian mission would help them get there. In the wake of his assassination, Richard Colvin accepted the risk to bring stabilization and reconstruction to a traumatized people. His voice, soft and precise with a trace British accent, quavers a little when he speaks of the woman whose husband disappeared, and for whom he could get no answer. It haunts him still.

Many of us are haunted by the assassination campaign that killed so many of the Afghans we worked with. As Collin observed, "I think there is a profound sadness from the cohort that was in Kandahar that last year with us. We saw our Afghan partners as colleagues we were working with. And suddenly they're no longer with us. In a very different world, they could have been our neighbours, or the person in the office next to you. All they did was stick their necks out for a better future. And that's tragic."

Summing up our collective experience, he said, "Sometimes international situations will quickly unravel even if the Canadian government does its very best. We were just another foreign force there for a matter of years while the Kandaharis viewed the conflict through a prism of centuries. We can make a difference, but it's extremely limited if we don't have a clear understanding of the situation at hand, the motivations that drive people, or the dilemmas they face."

# CONCLUSION

During a Fakeghanistan training session, when I was meeting my team for the first time, Jenny Hill asked, "Tim, why did you put your name forward for this?"

Caught by surprise, my only option was to be honest. "I didn't ask to go to Kandahar. I wanted to stay in Argentina." Nonetheless, my time as RoCK remains the high-water mark of my diplomatic career. It taught me things I could never have learned outside the blast furnace of that war.

Some of the benefits we delivered will endure. Water will still be flowing to irrigate Kandahari farmer's fields. Girls who are now literate will be forever changed and will retain that ambition to learn and achieve, even if it is brutally repressed for now. Thousands upon thousands escaped being disabled by polio. Better maternal health care saved and safeguarded the lives of countless mothers and children. But those billions of dollars did not produce a stable, democratic and prosperous province. Not even close.

I have thought long and hard about why peace in Afghanistan was unwinnable. This is what I think now, but maybe events will surprise us. Kandahar has surprised us before.

Afghan history left no space for a competent and legitimate modern government to take root and grow in Kandahar, with its unrelenting violence and endemic corruption. Nor were educated young leaders available to step forward in the face of a vicious assassination campaign against government workers. Good governance was caught in an uneven struggle against bad governance and it was hard, if not impossible, for us to tell the difference between good guys and bad guys.

The Taliban were rooted in their society, and we were the new-comers. Their behaviours, beliefs and hold on the society were incomprehensible to us. Information came in a series of explosive flashes that was impossible to understand in the short year left for our mission. We could not create social change in traditional Pashtun society when we were seen as another foreign force in a long line of them. Our theory of change depended on security making space for development and human rights. Those are two very soft and easy targets for a ruthless enemy in a cruel insurgency.

Peace was back-end loaded. Earlier opportunities for peace negotiations were not grasped, nor was peace among our objectives. Perhaps that was because the political courage was not there to sit down with the enemy, perhaps because we and our allies wanted a decisive victory too badly. When the US opened negotiations, fatigue and political expediency ruled. Security guarantees for the United States got the front seat. Reconstruction, development and women's rights fell off the back. The international community left Afghanistan *en masse* and the Taliban won.

In pride of place in Ottawa, in front of the National Gallery, stands Canada's monument to peacekeeping—three life-sized bronze Canadian soldiers, two men and a woman. They are in uniform and standing on broken concrete. Two are in berets, one erect and vigilant, looking into the distance with binoculars, another stooped on one knee calling in a report on a field radio. A soldier in a helmet and flak jacket has a rifle over his shoulder. Entitled "Reconciliation," the statue symbolizes the role peacekeeping plays in helping warring countries disengage.

Peacekeeping has an important place in Canada's history and identity that dates back to Lester Pearson, who developed a peace-keeping model to prevent the UK, France and Israel entering into armed conflict with Egypt over control of the Suez Canal. He was awarded the Nobel Peace Prize for his efforts.

The Afghanistan War Memorial is a stark and sombre contrast. It has been designed but not yet produced. The Veterans' Affairs website describes it this way:

> "The design, developed by Team Stimson, draws on elements of healing from the Medicine Wheel and takes the form of a circular, sacred space of safety, a "home base" of reflection, memory and contemplation. It is made up of four portals, where an interior area is the sanctuary where the fallen are remembered. Inscribed on the walls of three of the quadrants is the year, and names of the fallen and maple leaves, in several rows. The fourth southeast quadrant wall facing the direction of Afghanistan is dedicated to fallen Afghan Allies. In the centre, four bronze flak jackets stand draped on crosses—utilitarian yet poignant reminders of protection."

This is the design I voted for when Canadians were invited to voice their preferences. For me, the jackets, scuffed and frayed, scratched by the unforgiving landscape, convey the wear and tear on the soldiers tasked with securing strangers in a foreign land, and the wear and tear on the Canadian people and psyche from a campaign that ended in tragedy.

There is no victory here. Instead, the memorial is intended to create a place for Canadians to "honour and reflect, and to seek balance and healing." Once complete, it will be placed in front of the Canadian War Museum.

History delivers tragedies to test nations. Kandahar was the test for my generation of Canadians. Faced with crises for which we were not prepared, we reached into our Canadian values and found practical ways to work in humanitarian spaces and prevent torture. We found a way to partner with the government of Kandahar and push forward governance and development where security permitted. That security was hard won by Canadian, Afghan and US allies. With the KPRT, Canada innovated a new kind of organization that empowered civilian expertise from across our government with military security, mobility, intelligence and know-how. We were reminded that the Canadian forces are a proud part of our international reputation, national security and collective identity. We could do it again if we need to.

Kandahar taught me to be prepared for tragic outcomes and that war is an inescapable dimension of the human condition. It cost lives and dashed hopes; that is the price we paid together as a nation. The heavier burdens are carried on the shoulders of individual men, women and families, Canadian and Afghan, suffering from physical and psychological trauma. Families of Afghans who worked with Canada have been split asunder.

Canadian courage surfaced in Kandahar and made visible the heroes among us. It is in the darkest places that Canada's valour and values shine brightest.

# ACKNOWLEDGMENTS

This is a book of stories, shared by the contributors with intellectual honesty and emotional sincerity. I thank them for their candour, insight and heart. Their gift to me, and the readers, is to help us understand the meaning of the Afghanistan tragedy through the individual human experiences that result when political choices land on the unforgiving landscape of reality, and how they have been changed by Kandahar.

I am grateful to the members of the Canadian Forces who protected me and my colleagues in the course of our duties. Among the many benefits of being a Canadian, we are protected and represented by one of the best small armies in the world. Canadian Forces personnel are ready to fight and risk their lives for our country. It doesn't matter if they agree or disagree with the politics—they go. As citizens, our covenant with them is to always remember and honour their sacrifices for Canada.

I want to recognize the brave and dedicated Afghans who helped us, thereby binding their destiny to Canada. They carry a burden of grief for the homes and families they had to leave behind. I wish them every success in the hard and sometimes painful journey of settling in their new country. I am very glad they are now fellow Canadians.

Global Affairs permitted its employees to speak on the record with me about their experiences. This was a positive, constructive and healthy decision without which this book could not have been written. I am grateful for that permission and I take it as an expression of respect for the dedication and courage of Canadian diplomats and aid workers who served in Kandahar.

The constant support and editorial superpowers of Lynn Duncan and Kilmeny Denny of Tidewater Press made *Unwinnable Peace* possible. They shepherded complex, confusing and multifaceted experiences into a meaningful and coherent story about a landmark chapter in the history of Canada's international policy.

After a while, this writer becomes blind to his own words and deaf to his own voice. For me, the Buenos Aires English Writers Group provided the fresh eyes and ears I needed to find my way through this maze of a story. Thank you, fellow writers, for your kind criticism and companionship in this solitary pursuit we share.

# CONTRIBUTORS
## AND THEIR POSITIONS IN KANDAHAR

Howard Coombs, Counterinsurgency Advisor

Richard Colvin, Political Director, KPRT

Collin Goodlet, Chief of Political Intelligence, ASIC

Mike Detroit, (not real name)

Jess Dutton, KPRT Director

Greg Galligan, Political Deputy Director, KPRT

Ahmad Habibi, Brigadier General, Brigade commander,
  first brigade 205th Corps

Terry Hackett, Head of Correctional Service Canada team

Bernard Haven, Development Officer, RC South and KPRT

Barbara Hendrick, Deputy Director, Development

Jenny Hill, Development Advisor

Pam Isfeld, Political Advisor to Commander of RC South

Joffre LeBlanc, District Stabilization Officer, Panjwai

Philip Lupul, Political Director, KPRT

Joe McAllister, Commander of Civilian Police Contingent

Dean Milner, General, Commander of Task Force Kandahar

Vic Park, Commander, Civilian Police Contingent

Ben Rowswell, RoCK

Bushra Saeed-Khan, Political Officer

Maryam Sahar, Interpreter

Ahmad Shoaib (aka Rambo), Interpreter

Katherine Heath-Eves, Strategic Communications Officer,
  KAF and KPRT

Adam Sweet, Public Diplomacy Officer, KPRT

Ehsan Ullah, Director, Afghan Canadian Community Centre

Tooryalai Wesa, Governor of Kandahar Province

# ABOUT THE AUTHOR

A policy leader and career diplomat, Tim has been at the forefront of Canadian diplomacy in Latin America, Afghanistan, the Middle East and Africa. He has served as Ambassador to Colombia and to Argentina and Paraguay.

In 1998, he served as the first Representative of Canada (RoCK) to the Palestinian Authority and in 2011, he was the last Representative of Canada in Kandahar, Afghanistan.

His career includes accreditation to Barbados, Ethiopia, Somalia, Sudan, Eritrea, Kenya, Rwanda, Burundi and Uganda. Among his other roles are Chairman of the Kimberley Process to Ban Conflict Diamonds (2004). Following his diplomatic career, he worked as a consultant on human rights issues connected to mining.

Tim is a recipient of the Canadian Treasury Board's Award of Excellence in the Public Service for his leadership on Canada's humanitarian assistance to Palestinian children affected by conflict. He has been awarded three medals by Canada's Governor General: the Commemorative Medal of the 125th Anniversary of Confederation, the Queen's Jubilee Medal, and the Operational Service Medal.

Now dedicated to writing, *Unwinnable Peace* follows his debut political thriller, *Moral Hazards*.

Tim lives with his wife Fatima in Minaki, Ontario. He is proud of his daughters, Natasha and Jena, sons-in-law Mads and Corrado and his four grandchildren, Nico, Luca, Theo and Josefine.

# Index